Little Duke Boy

From Poverty to Purpose

Written by Tennille Chaffin

Little Duke Boy

Published by Chocolate Readings via Kindle Direct Publishing

www.chocolatereadings.com

ISBN-13: 9781709490453

Publisher's Note

Dedication

With all glory and praise, I want to thank God for keeping his hands on me throughout my entire lifetime. For covering my children, transforming my mindset and blessing my mother with the ability to get where she has gone before my eyes. No matter how bleak things seemed and were at times, a way was made possible. Thank you for speaking to me through dreams, visions and portents. God never left me without guidance and direction no matter the season or situation. To Debbie Dent thank you for showing me what reinventing yourself is all about and what the definition of being focused and keeping that heat up off you is all about! You led by example showing us that no matter the age it's never too late. Thank you for inspiring me through your daily strength and faith in the Lord. Thank you to my siblings for putting up with my poor decision makings and all the ego driven antics over the last 40 years. Grandma Evelyn Dent rest in peace I always think of you. Thank you, Monica, for approaching me that night and becoming my wife and loyal friend. There isn't any word that can explain what we share and experienced together. To a host of family that has supported me at some time or another from my adolescent years to now, thank you and continue breaking the generational curse. Thank you, Jessica Lee Ann, @chocolatereadings for being available and helping me see this masterpiece through. To every fallen soldier in Duquesne PA where it all started Cousin Antwan Lawrence, Corey Snap, Eric E.T Taylor, Shon Rooskie, Cousin Harold, Mont Neal, Bowie City, Swamp Fox, Lil Ty Coleman, Erie Pirl, Ms. Lockey Pirl, Uncle Daryl, Chilly Fat, Lil Beenie Kelly, Uncle Jimmy, Aunt Betsy, Billy Joe, all the fallen soldiers down Larimer Ave where I stomped at for some time Rest In Peace…… to anyone I forgot or didn't mention you know the vibes…….. Thank you to everyone also who I didn't mention that has my best interest at heart and always keep it 100 and stay tuned in, I'll never tune you out!!!!! Thank you to everyone who believed in my vision and all my supporters and readers. One day we will see this on the big screen. STAY FOCUSED AND KEEP THAT HEAT UP OFF YOU …………………

Chapter One

The Beginning

"Stop it! Stop it, Algae! Get the heck off of him; you crazy son of a gun. Call the ambulance! Call 911, Dawn! Billy! Billy Joe, are you alright?"

My mother's screams could be heard throughout the entire apartment. Those are the screams that woke me up. Getting a glance of my big brother covered in blood on the bed, droplets in every room, covering the linoleum floors, is all that I remember. And screaming. Everyone was screaming.

My Uncle Algae was special far back as I can remember. Some people say he was destined to play football for Ohio State; that is until someone spiked his drink. Not sure if you remember "Alfa & Seeka" the Samoan Warriors. Well, he claimed that he was one. He was about that life. He'd have his big LL Cool J radio, Newport's, and a bottle of Tiger Rose posted up on the Ave, Priscilla Ave, listening to some old school funk.

But on this particular night, he was on my bro with a frying pan. A small, black cast iron skillet was gripped into his midsized heavy hands. Hands with long fingernails that will cut you like a knife.

Finally, the ambulance arrived. My bro got carried out on a stretcher. My uncle was screaming something about my brother taking money out of my Gram's purse. I still don't believe that, though. Now if he accused him of stealing someone's hoagie, I'd believe that!

Billy's bed was drenched, and my sister Dawn was stuck with the task of cleaning it up. Then she was told to, "flip the darn thing over."

Uncle Algae was arrested maybe 60 times but was always out within hours. I remember one day when I was a bit older, he got into it with a Duquesne police officer and bit the officer's ear off. Unc was well respected and feared down the Jets.

We were one of the ninety-six families that resided down the 'Jets' Cochrandale projects. Two buildings. One-way in. One way out. Each building had four entrances in the front and four in the back. A4-B14 was my address. Building A 4th entrance B 2nd floor 14 – 4th door.

Things happened very fast in the projects. It seemed everything and everybody was moving faster than they should've been. Seeing way too much at a young age can leave children with devastating consequences.

We had family feuds and all. I mean all-out brawls. I must admit that there is one that I started. I grew up the youngest of three. Yes, they said I got away with way more! Maybe they were right. My brother is nine years older than me, and my sister, Dawn, five years older. So I'd say that I was 4 years old when I was awakened to the aggravated assault on my big brother committed by Uncle Algae.

I remember seeing him the next morning all swollen up with a golf ball-sized eye, and bandages around his head. He motivated me because he was still moving around the next day as if nothing had happened.

I didn't see Mom until the wee hours of the following morning when I awoke to, "*I got my mind made up come on you can get it, girl, anytime say what? Tonight is fine. If you want my money you better, make it as good as honey.*" That was Instafunk 1979 "I Got My Mind Made Up."

I sat up in the bed drenched with sweat from the summer heat. Throughout the air was the stench of cigarettes and alcohol, or some sort of cheap wine. The little inquisitive kid I was, slid out of the bed. Slowly turning the knob of my bedroom, well our bedroom door, I slid my skinny frame through the cracked door, got on my knees, and crawled toward the corner of the wall in the hallway. As I wiped the sleep out of my eyes,

I took a long gaze into the living room. Just through the long-beaded partition, I saw some bald light-skinned man with a huge smile on his face and heard my momma's voice very vaguely repeating the word Bubby over and over. As soon as I started to crawl forward, I got yanked by my underwear. An immediate wedgy followed in one motion.

It was my sister, Dawn, grabbing me up and saying, "Get back in the bed and don't move. Go to bed we have school soon." *School?* I thought to myself. Oh yes, school! I can't wait.

My first day of school. Seems like it was just five minutes later that I was being awakened and told to go brush my teeth and get ready for school. I echoed with a whiny whimper, "Alright, I'm hungry," as I went into the bathroom wiping and blowing my nose. My bro was gone already. He started his day much earlier. My sister was directing me to get dressed, be quiet, and to stop whining about my cereal, as it was already waiting for me. I cleaned up, got dressed, and headed into the tiny kitchen. I sat down at the round table and watched my sister take a white box and pour a white powdered substance into our Kool-Aid container. She then turned the spigot on and ran water into it also. As she stirred quickly with gentle cautious strokes, it soon formed into a milky grayish-white liquid. That's what I was born to know as milk. And yes, I noticed the difference when we finally became fortunate enough to purchase blue or red plastic top liquid form. What Pac say? "It ain't easy being me." I tore them cornflakes up, and I was off to my first day of school.

As soon as I stepped on the concrete outside of our apartment building, there was the "Dirty Pimp" Mikey the worse kid ever. He was the most ruthless, the funniest dude in our building. He was the first to do every double dare we called out and had an attitude - so you knew you'd be fighting him after just ten minutes of hanging with him for that day.

Most adults he respected after he called you every name in the book. As he grew up, he became calmer and more respectful after he finally got his first girlfriend at 25 years old. Then *she* caught the vapors the majority of the time.

Today, he was out singing, dancing, and making us all laugh on our way up the back steps toward school. By the time we all made it up the back steps, the Dirty Pimp's older brother, Tone, was chasing him trying to fight him because he played with him so much. Tone was more of a chill kid. It seemed as if we all had the same shoes. Nike Air Force 1's, which was released early '82 by Nike or the Diadora Borg Elite that released in 1981. I wondered if some white man rode up in the projects and sold a 100 pair of the same sneakers or if we all shopped at Big Lots or what?

My first day of school was like Christmas actually, being that it was one of the few times of year that I received anything new. I was a quiet, laid back, very observant young child. I had quite a few nicknames. Turtle was one because I seemed to run the slowest. Maybe I was just being cautious and observant and staying aware of my surroundings. First Aid was another nickname that it seemed only two people called me. That's Ron Reid and Gadgey. They were a couple of older guys that were more my brother's age, maybe my sister's age. Another couple from the 96 families down the Jets. I say down the Jets because it seems that it was the very bottom of the whole Duquesne. It was almost like our Ancestors were instructed to shovel and cut out a huge portion of a mountain and then they stuck us at the very bottom. The only thing around us was a steel mill that was walking distance and a local store, along with a few bars. Stanley's bar was the one I remembered the most because some nights we'd sneak down there and hustle the hustlers and pimps out of a quarter or two. Maybe even a dollar if we ran across Yerbie or even Swamp Fox! As I got older Turtle and First Aid turned into a lot of other names.

After our first day of school, we all were playing outside 'til the night lights came on, some a bit longer, quite a few much sooner. We would run around playing every game possible - It Tag, Cooties, 'Engine Engine Number 9 if the train jumps off the track'. Yeah, all kinds of catch and release games, Hide and Seek, 7/11 (seven kisses/eleven humps). Yes, girls played with us also.

Just before the streetlights came on, Speedy John Pirl started mocking the parents, teasing the kids as they stuck their heads out the front kitchen windows screaming, "TONE TONE. MIKEY. Let's go boys." "Ron, Reese, Telly. Let's go". "SLICC get 'cha yellow behind in here NOW. You got 10 seconds…9, 8, 7…let's go!"

Sure enough, in a matter of minutes, the roll call began and the echoes of bouncing basketballs and screams of playful joy were over. Bathe. Lights out. And up to another day doing the same.

I can remember it being so hot in our apartment I'd stare at the window and wonder why they even made them. Seems we would've been better off without windows at all. We hardly ever closed them even in the wintertime when we used our stove to heat the place. Burners on the stove going full blast and the oven cranked up to the highest setting. I guess the windows were kept open to keep us from passing out from the carbon fumes. I look at the news now and see how many deaths occur from things of such and just praise the Lord we survived that phase.

The next few days weren't much different, except for the fact I was wearing a neck brace now. Well, I was supposed to be wearing one all the time since I got hurt.

One particular day, I decided I was going to play fastpitch with the older kids. We'd play pickup games constantly. Baseball was just about all of our favorites; it was mine. Our home plate was the wall of our building. We'd paint, chalk, spray paint, do whatever we had to make sure every base was official. No helmets or any protection. We were playing HARDBALL, regardless of what any grown-up said about our safety. As long as nobody was fighting, we could get away with just about anything. Wasn't any fighting this evening, just screams from First Aid.

As I was batting, Flash threw a pitch and it landed directly on the left side of my neck. The kid was 4 ½ years older than me and it showed with the power that was behind the pitch. I immediately dropped the aluminum bat and my whole body followed. I screamed and cried until I got home from the hospital that evening. I was now wearing a huge neck brace that I wasn't supposed to take off. The very next day after getting teased and feeling handicapped, I decided every chance I got away from home, that I wasn't going to wear it. I eventually hid it, lost it… something. Because I stopped wearing the brace, I had developed a permanent tilt in my neck. My injury didn't heal properly, and I favored leaning it to the less resistant side. That by far didn't stop my love for baseball. I played every chance I got. I even played for our little league team. So much talent came out of the Jets for baseball it was unbelievable. We all shared a passion for the sport.

Every day it seemed we all started walking to practice up Polish Hill. Most of us were on the same team. The Giants & Angels our bigger team. I earned so many trophies and MVP's; I was picked to go and play many night games because I excelled in the sport and paid my dues on the small team during the earlier game. With being able to play every position, I'd get picked to help out somewhere during the major league game under the night lights. It seemed every game was jammed packed with grown-ups and kids running around everywhere.

I remember getting my first real glove, an all-leather Dwight Gooden. That's when I *really* knew that my mother believed that I was a good baseball player. Up until that point, it seemed she paid very little attention to my dreams. Moms was always on the go. I spent more time being watched by my sister than anyone else. She made sure I ate and was safe. She even beat some boys up for me.

Dawn was quiet, wore glasses, kinda thick lens ones, had a jerry curl that left dark spots on her neck collar and pillowcases. Anywhere you saw a dark stain, you knew Dawn was there. She was always focused, though. Always working as far back as I can remember. She would sell 10 cent icy cups, which were flavored Kool-Aid frozen inside little Styrofoam cups. And she put together the best meals, whether they were syrup sandwiches, a peanut butter, OR a jelly sandwich. We never seemed to have both at the same time. Or even a nice toasted cheese bread. A few slices of thick sliced government cheese in the long rectangular brown box with extra thick plastic you had to fight with to pull up off the cheese. She'd slice it just perfect and place the cheese on one slice of bread and then place it at the very bottom of the oven broiler for which it seemed like an eternity some nights but was probably more like two minutes tops. Maybe I was just that greedy or hungry as ever. Real talk, whatever she whipped up seemed like it was the best meal ever.

No matter what, we very seldom, if ever, ran out of the big block cheese. Now, on the other hand, rice was scarce with a meal. We seemed to never have it when she made kielbasa and creamed corn. Hot dogs were my all-time favorite. Fried, boiled, raw, cut-up, no bread or ketchup, whatever. One thing was for sure though, we ate.

Then, there were the late nights I'd wait up for my Aunt Monica to come in with that delicious, sweet sauce, lightly browned, mouth-watering personal pan pizza from Pizza Hut. This pizza was amazing! I've developed a love for pasta and pizza because of this lady. I was so grateful to have her thinking of me and my siblings every other evening or so that she worked bringing it home for us. I couldn't wait to hear her voice and distinct laugh. She still to this very day will light up a room, always happy. I don't think I've ever seen her unhappy.

Maybe that was in part because Uncle Quick was always the same way and a good man to her and everyone else. Father, good basketball player, and coach, community-oriented, motivational speaker, and much more. At parties, they'd be on the dance floor all night. Just happy, joyful folks. Their children Drea, Care Bear, Little Quick, and Jahla, all grew up to be happy productive adults that started their own families.

Praise the Lord for the blessings continuing to see generational curses being broken. Breaking chains is what Pastor Edmunds would say.

Family Affair

My grandmother, Evelyn Dent, had seven children. Uncle Jimmy, Aunt Jackie, my mom Debbie, Uncle Rickie, Aunt Robin, Uncle Algae, and Aunt Monica They said I looked just like my Uncle Jimmy. (Maybe that was why Gram said I was her fav!). I never remembered him though, because they said he died before I was born. Aunt Jackie had Ron, Scotty, Dina, and Keith. Keith was just a few years older than me. They lived about fifteen minutes away in another Government-subsidized housing, Whitaker. Uncle Ronnie always held a job. He took good care of Aunt Jackie. Luxury compared to what I was accustomed to. I spent time over there as well on weekends. Occasionally, I ate good, had fun, and felt the love. Thank you for those blessings.

We were a very tight family; we were all we had and staying connected wasn't an option. I watched how all of my Aunts and Uncles chipped in and always made sure my grandmother was alright as well as each of their siblings. A valuable lesson that I would carry with me the rest of my living days. Family Over Everything. We all we got, besides the Lord

Chapter Two

What More Can I Say

Screams fill the air and then I hear Dirty Meech saying, "It's out on you Ock, and if you say another word I'm'a knock you the heck out right here!" Big Ock was tall and a heavyweight. He was from Burns heights, sort of a Cochrandale Jets rival at times. Meech, on the other hand, was from the Jets. Big Ock, being the big guy he was, started shouting back and before you knew it, he was lying flat on his back after hearing a loud thump.

After the crowd slowly faded off into different groups, Telly, Speedy, Slicc, Clarkie G and I, headed back into the Jets. "Hey, ya'll want to make a video?" Clarkie G had his new video recorder in his hand. He rewound the tape and played the knockout Meech had put on Big Ock. We laughed and laughed, as Ms. Shirly came walking up. "Come on, Lamar!" she shouted in a jittery tone. "Come on. Only five minutes. Just give me one now and I'll get ready. Come on." He then reached into his pouch that was strapped around his waistline. He unzipped it, fiddled with this medicine bottle and opened the top. He turned his back to us, well attempted to anyhow. As I got a glance, being the observant child I was, I noticed he poured what looked like a bunch of little yellowish, ivory soap pieces into his hand. With one stroke, he then slid all the pieces back into the bottle, except for two tiny itty-bitty pieces. He gave her one, and she begged for the other one. He said, “No, I’ll give it to you after you’re done.” She agreed and said, “Let’s go, meet me at the back door. I’ll go up the front way and open the back door for ya’ll.” He turned to us and said, “Let’s go. And before we go in here, none of ya’ll better say a word.”

We all walked toward the back door of the B Building, one by one trying to go unnoticed. We all eventually made it to the third floor. As I entered last behind Slicc, I stood in awe at this lady, edging us on saying, “Come on, hurry up!” I looked in disbelief. I thought to myself, *you’re only 10 years old, Clabo.*

Clarkie G stood with the camera in hand edging some on, some complied as others didn’t.

Always remember what’s done in the dark comes to the light most of the time.

As a few weeks passed by, we became the whisper amongst the neighborhood and grown-ups. My mother didn’t seem to know because she never said anything. I don’t remember getting reprimanded, put it that way. One day I was in the A1 Building on the second floor about to knock on Mickey Moe’s door. I could hear this lady talking loud through the door. Ms.

White was saying, “Oh my goodness, that boy. Clarkie G, what in the world are you doing with these kids?” From that day forward, I knew Clarkie G wasn’t to be trusted. I turned around after I was done eavesdropping. As I exited the building, my brother was walking home from playing basketball down Wylie. He had a brand-new basketball in his hand. I begged to see the ball all the way home until he finally gave in and said, “Don’t leave my ball outside.” I walked off dribbling, fantasizing as if I was Dr. J until Slicc and Speedy John ran off waving for a pass calling my name out.

As Slicc was doing fancy moves dribbling at the top court in the project’s playground, the gray Saab with dark tinted windows pulled up again. This time he rolled the passenger window down and called out in a deep stern voice, “Clarkie G!” Clarkie G then made a faint whisper, “Man I’m giving this back. He just gave it to me four hours ago!”

As we directed our attention to the nice sparkling new car, Clarkie G returned after a brief talk, smiling. We asked, “Who was that?” He quickly said, “That’s crazy-ass Beany Sco. And Slicc, he said he heard about you handling your business with Chuck Chuck and heard you are moving quick and have potential.” Slicc then looked with fear and confusion while asking Telly for a cigarette. His yellow two front buck teeth were all you noticed. Slicc and Clarkie G then conversed for a little bit before being overheard saying, “Yeah, he gave me two ounces for $1,600 apiece, fish scales, too! I'll tell him when he comes back in a couple of hours."

Sure enough like clockwork, he came back in a couple of hours, which only seemed like 30 minutes. This time you could hear music playing. *You been waiting and debating for so long cause I make a lot of money and your boyfriend don't. LL Cool J is hard as hell. Double L Rock the Bells* banged from the Kenwood system. A very tall, light-skinned, muscular built guy exited the gray Saab and walked up and said what's up to everyone. He grabbed the ball and shot an airball. He then reached in his pocket and pulled out a wad of crispy green bills and gave all the kids five and ten-dollar bills. He handed Clarkie G a brown folded bag and said, "I'll see you on the first". Clarkie G then nodded his head and walked away whispering, "Man, it's already September 30th. Sco is crazy as heck."

I headed home and walked into our apartment without the new Spalding basketball my brother had allowed me to play with. And it was immediately evident that he noticed as he screamed, "Where's my darn ball?" I don't know why, but I instantly started crying and said, "I don't know. Out there," and pointed out the window with snot drooling from my nose as I licked and wiped it away with the back of my hand. My sister calmly intervened and said, "Go get your butt in the tub. Get bathed and ready for bed." As I bathed and lay in my twin bed still sniffling, it came to my mind in an instance that I saw the ball rolling down the middle of the road as we stood directing our attention to Sco as he had conducted business.

The following day, I was sitting at home watching WWE wrestling, Big John Stud vs Hulk Hogan, when Billy Joe walked in with what seemed like a fat lip and clothes dirtier than the usual from just not being able to hand wash them fast enough properly. He also had his basketball clutched tightly in his arm. He looked my way, made eye contact and then lunged the ball at me. I closed my eyes and put my hands up only to find that the ball somehow slipped through partially between my hand and made contact with my nose. Instantly my eyes became watery. Not from crying, but the force of the ball hitting the bridge of my nose caused a sharp burning, painful sensation. He then screamed out, "If you let my ball roll down Wylie again, I'm going whoop your butt! Don't touch my stuff anymore!" Then he went on to say that he got into a fight with some guy from Burns Heights over the ball. I'm thinking, *'his STUFF?' Does he mean everything?!?* I just sat with a stare and deep thoughts of, *does my big brother love his basketball more than he loves me?*

Well, I'm going to see if he does. I then looked out the window in the kitchen so I could get a better view to see if my friends were out at our usual hangout, and sure enough, they were. I then tiptoed to see where my bro was. He was in the bedroom on the phone. Had I looked down at the phone cord stretched from the living room to our bedroom across the floor, I wouldn't have tripped and made a ton of noise to cause him to look out the bedroom at me. Just as he did and screamed something at me, I said, "Screw you!" and grabbed his basketball and ran for the door. He was partially dressed so he didn't run after me. I stood outside and called his name until he eventually stuck his bowling ball head out the window. I said, "Look! Screw this ball!" and rolled it down the road. He chased me all over the projects then around the back stairs, and into 'the path' that led up into the other side of town. He pulled me by my sweatshirt down the road until we found the ball. After we got the ball, he told me to stop crying and asked why I did that. I told him because he hurt my feelings and I felt like he cared for the ball more than he does me. He explained that no way was that true and gave me a high five and talked to me until we got home.

Seemed as if that was the most, he had ever talked to me in my lifetime. I'm thinking, *now, what else can I do to get his attention like that.* After we talked, he went back into the house. I sat on the front steps and watched as the gray Saab pulled up playing Eric B and Rakim. The big bald guy got out of his car walked around to the other side and approached this guy. I noticed a shorthand gesturing conversation and then he went back to the car with a slow limp and grabbed a huge silver pistol with a long barrel and headed back to where the guys were standing. He then said something with a quick hand gesture again with the other hand and before my eyes, he pointed it at this guy's head and BOOM! In an instant, it looked as if the guy's head exploded and the echo could be felt in your stomach from the blast. Everyone started screaming and running. I sat in a daze, staring at the big guy as he calmly walked back to his car and pulled away slowly. Maybe five minutes later, the police showed up as everyone seemed to surround the lifeless body. I'll never forget the stream of blood that ran down the street I had just walked up. As the old station wagon pulled up with Allegheny Coroners in big bold letters printed on the side, I watched as they chalked around the body then zipped the lifeless body up into a body bag.

Soon after, the fire trucks pulled up and unwound their long tan hose and hooked it up to the yellow fire hydrant. One of them turned it on with a super huge wrench and immediately started washing all the blood down the street, a scene I'll never forget. A couple of days later, Beenie Sco was arrested, eventually convicted, and sentenced to a life term.

Later that evening after everything calmed down and went back to our normal setting, Clarkie G, Slicc, and Shon Rooskie walked up. We talked about what happened earlier. Slicc said, "That muthasucka is crazy. I knew it! I'm keeping everything he gave me now it's on!" I chimed in, "Keeping what?" He replied, "Fish scales, Clabo, that's what!" Then he pulled out a sandwich baggie full of little tarnished white individually wrapped things.

Ms. Shirly walked up and said, "Come on let me get just one itty bitty bump. Come on please Slicc. Tell him G. Tell him. Please?"

"Bunk that! Put me in the game coach!" Rooskie yelled out with a grin. "It's like that? I want to eat. It's that easy?" Slicc opened the huge sandwich bag with his big yellow stained teeth from all the cigarette smoking he'd been doing for several years as a pre-teen. when he opened it, he put his high yellow hand into the baggie and gave Rooskie ten little bags and said, "Give me $140 back". With that grin, Rooskie accepted and soon was off on his way.

Chapter Three

Shorty Wanna Be a Thug

Saturday afternoon. I'm pitching with two runners on base, one out, the count is three balls and two strikes. The crowd is chanting, "Clabo! Clabo! Clabo! Clabo!" in a slow, steady rhythm. My teammates instructed me to throw a strike for the second out. I threw a slow curveball right over the left side of the plate as the umpire called ball four and signaled the batter to first base. The Giants were playing against our rivals, the Tigers. Now the bases were loaded, and for the Tigers, my cousin Moe Joe was at-bat. It was a straight love-hate relationship playing against him. While in the tournaments, I loved having him on my team because he was fast, and strong, and could hit home runs. I was skinny and could only hit inside the parkers, never a home run. I hated it when I had to hit or pitch against him, though. Same for another kid, Chris, who was up after him. Now, I'm sweating. I pulled my black and yellow hat with a G on it and wiped my head. My catcher C.Y. signaled that he wanted me to throw a fastball. The crowd continued to chant my name. I nodded yes and delivered a 64-mph fastball only to have him swing and hit the ball with a loud TING! The ball was up in the air and caught just short of the fence by Rodney, which he quickly threw to second base and Sweat Pea tagged the runner out as he tried to hurry back and slide back into the base. We all jumped, screamed, and celebrated as we had just won our second divisional title. This would be our last game together playing little league baseball. I enjoyed every moment. I could have gone far and been the next Josh Gipson or Roberto Clemente.

As it turned out, the very next spring I'd be feeding my cousin Rueben's pet raccoon and sleeping next to Great Danes that were just as tall as I was. We soon moved out of the projects after having a yellow notice posted on our door that read "10-day notice to vacate."

At the time, I didn't know why, but I was happy it wouldn't be far away. We were only moving up the street to Crawford Ave. right across the street from another projects, Burns Heights. My cousin Reuben lived on the other end in a big house that his mom and stepdad purchased. Cousin Marcia, Reuben's mom, was awesome. They had a big home. And kids to play with. I mean, her kids and the communities' kids. Her husband, Daryl, was a devoted churchgoer by day and would curse up a storm by night. They had go-carts, minibikes, jukeboxes, and all the vending equipment. Ms. Pac Man. The real arcade games. Their home was the super fun house. Daryl made us work to play, though; which I look at now and still thank him for teaching me such valuable traits and understandings of life.

During midget football season the whole team would stay at his house the night before the games. We just had got our league back going. Both of my cousins, Moe Joe and Reuben, were running backs. Reuben would run everybody over, make it just short of the goal line, and then fumble. We'd laugh and we'd call him, Fumblelitist! If that's even a word. casually I started to hang in Burns Heights and at my cousin Reuben's and then all over. I now had friends all over not just in school or the Jets or at baseball.

One day, I came home from school only to find two white men with crew cuts and Army uniforms on sitting at our kitchen table. The one guy was sitting in the broken chair, the chair that if you didn't know about it being broken, you'd soon find out, as all my friends did. Eventually, I sat down and just looked and waited for it to happen, but for some reason, it never occurred. What did occur and became known was that my big brother would be joining the Army and getting shipped off to Germany in two weeks. *Germany?* I thought. "Germany, I had just read about that place in social studies class" I cried when I heard this news. My big bro is leaving home. Who's going to have my back now? Will a man come and hurt me or try to hurt my mom?

After all, my brother did try to fight Bubby one day when he and my mom were arguing, and she packed his bags up. From that day on for the next two weeks in May until school was dismissed for summer break, I followed my big bro around everywhere. I would wait outside the bathroom while he was inside. I think he started realizing just how much I loved him. On that very last evening as his packed bags sat near the front door he blasted 'How Can I Move the Crowd, First of All, Ain't No Mistakes Allowed' by Eric B and Rakim. We stayed up all night long. The entire family showed up, and a host of friends for Billy Joe's farewell to serve the country, leaving behind his newborn child Little Bill.

The next morning, I cried and hugged him, as he gave me a big hug. and his cassette tape of the new Rakim. "Don't lose it. Every time you think of me, play this tape. And be good and take care of Mom and Dawn." In my eleven-year-old head, the thought of him saying 'take care of mom and Dawn' played over and over asking myself 'how am I going to do that?'

In a blink, he was gone. Dawn was now sixteen and working after school at someplace in the next town over. She caught the bus straight after school to work and wouldn't get home until 10 or 11 p.m. During the summer, that wasn't so bad because I'd go eat the summer breakfast and lunch at the Burns Heights' Center. Since she wasn't preparing meals much, Mom was hardly around and when she was, she was moody or sleeping or half-sleep sometimes nodding off. It seemed like she was ignoring me most times when she was awake because she would be stuck on an old western or King Kong movie. So now I had a lot of free time to do whatever and that's exactly what I slowly started doing, whatever.

Summer had arrived, and my birthday was soon approaching. Unfortunately, it was the worst birthday ever that I could remember. I wanted some new shoes, but instead, I got $25 in a card. I did get to have some friends over for ice cream and cake, though.

Rodney became an almost everyday friend. We found out his mom was doing bad things and didn't give him much except some essentials he needed, but no wants. So he'd steal from corner stores. He'd get away with stealing canned goods, Kool-Aid and all. I took notice and slowly started doing the same thing. He'd stay over my house until my mom started noticing, she'd say he couldn't stay, but we had a plan. "Go out the front and climb back in my window. She won't know." I started having a full stomach for sure! I was just a little hungry kid trying to make it. I only got one chance so I gotta take it!

A Valuable Lesson

Luckily for me, I didn't have to steal for too long. I was offered my first job. Uncle Daryl was offering me, Reuben, and Rodney a job carrying vending equipment, setting up booths and making snow cones, cotton candy, and funnel cakes. I loved this job! We made nachos and cheese and all. We worked long hours from 6 am to 9 pm we'd be at all the big events: The Annual Three Rivers Regatta, the Rib Cookoff, and all the smaller events in between held in downtown Pittsburgh. Afterward, late at night, he would count all of the money in front of us. We had to help sort ones, fives, tens, and twenties. I remember him counting over $7,000 from one day's work. Then he gave us all the ones, which between the three of us was only $45 apiece. Yes, he was working with us kids just as somebody must have worked him at some point prior. I remember Reuben being so mad at him for that, that he said, "Watch what I do tomorrow. Watch!" I asked, "Cuz, what you going to do?" to which he replied, "I'mma take mines, you better get yours!"

The next day came, and we were busy as ever working. I glanced over at Reuben one time as he tucked a good bit of money in his sweatpants and smiled at me. I couldn't do that though; they were too good to me. That became my second home for a few months. I'd never steal from someone that's like family. On the other hand, I understood where my cousin was coming from because Uncle Daryl was also very, very strict on Reuben.

Reuben was the oldest, so he made him do everything from dishes to taking care of the dogs, the raccoon and whatever other pets they had. Also, cleaning and maintaining the equipment, and the minibikes. After this day's work at the event, we did our same routine; counted money and put the equipment up, being it was the last day of the event. Daryl gave us $115 each and ordered 5 pizzas, and when the pizza man showed up at the door, he made us pitch in to pay for it!

Afterward, Reuben pulled all of his money out that he had tucked away. It was over $400. He gave me and Rodney $25 each. We went shopping the next day. We caught the 61C-bus downtown and shopped. We caught another bus to the mall on our little boy missions

Before My Eyes

One day after school, we were walking home and decided to head to my apartment for a minute so I could put my play shoes on. As soon as I got through the door, noticing water on the kitchen floor along with the sound of water running

I walked toward the bathroom and saw my mother lying in the bathtub passed out with the water running with an orange and clear plastic needle stuck in her arm dangling outside the tub. I screamed, "MOM!" but got no response. I ran back outside in a panic. Rodney, yelled, "What's wrong?" Explaining while crying that my mom was passed out and didn't respond to me. He then instructed me to call 9-1-1. He tried calling 9-1-1 on our house phone but kept getting a blank line. The phone was shut off from nonpayment.

As we ran back out, my sister was walking in. Not sure how or why as she was supposed to be at work. We told her about my mom. She darted outside the back door and into Skyy's house, the local barber. She was screaming emphatically, as they called 9-1-1. In the nick of time, the ambulance and police were inside my house looking around as my mom layout on the stretcher. My sister jumped in the back of the ambulance as it pulled away in a hurry. I remember the sound of the sirens going steady.

The word around town spread pretty fast that Ms. Deb overdosed on heroin. Something called "China White." I soon put together something I overheard in the projects while ear hustling near the yum yum tree. Well, I assumed after hearing the conversation in the near site of the local drug dealers' topics. However, sometime later, I did ask my mother where she purchased that lethal jolt at. She said, "Well, from my boyfriend," which was some older guy in the city Hill District that went by the name Shank.

Shank was an old school gangsta/hustler from way back. She went on to say Shank sold speedballs on the Hill District and had them bagged into red, blue, and yellow balloons looking like super tiny M&Ms. She went on to say she asked, "If it's your will Lord," then she went into Shank's stash and proceeded to the bathroom, syringes on hand readily available due to the fact she was a diabetic. It was nothing but normal to see her shoot up CC's of insulin into her arms and legs. Shank would leave before I left for school and wouldn't return until late in the evening. That was the normal routine of a gangsta that was selling dope in the city but living far away in the suburbs. We never really talked much to one another. It was like we had our greetings to a mere head nod as to just say what's up. He wasn't flashy with a big car or jewelry or anything, but I did take notice to the shiny pistol he kept nearby wrapped inside a red handkerchief that the gangbangers in California wore to cover their face. He never yelled or even raised his voice but being an enabler to my mother left a very bitter taste in my mouth.

I had previously overheard them talking one evening while they sat in their bedroom bagging up the narcotics. She was begging him to give her some for her friend, Ms. Linda. "We just need a couple more for our party this evening. I'mma sell six but we're going to need four for us." I could vaguely hear him reply in a burly grumble, "Alright, alright got darn." Mom's reply and tone of voice changed in an instant, "Oh, I need you to leave the money for the light bill." I then tiptoed away quietly without a screech to be heard. As I walked back towards the back door, I grabbed a twenty-dollar bill off the top of the mountain of cash that was in a man's pouch that was zipped partially closed.

From that day forward, I felt in my heart that I didn't like Shank. As I exited the house and asked Rodney if he wanted one of the little snack cakes I was about to start eating, he replied, "Naw, I'm about to fire this joint up I just got off VO."

VO was the barber's cousin he would sit outside the homemade barbershop and drink 40 ounces of beer all day, which was also my backyard and steps to the duplex apartment we shared. We walked and laughed as he tried to light the matches one after another with little success until in an instant, he took off running. Naturally, I just took off running behind him. We dipped between two houses, ran through backyards, and hopped over a fence into Burns Heights. We made it over the back hill and into Reuben's backyard. Out of breath and full of laughter I asked, "What happened?" He said, "We gotta stay ready, gotta stay on point, gotta big game tomorrow." We play Greenfield.

Reuben soon appeared from the side of his house with the little smirk on his face he always had. Informing us that they were getting ready for Bible study. Bible study was sometimes held in his living room. Daryl would invite any kid who wanted to join and learn the Word. They also owned a church. So, from staying with my cousin it quickly became part of my routine to learn the Word of God. We soon were instructed to call each other Brother Daryl, Brother Reuben, Brother Clabo, and Brother…whoever.

Daryl played a very influential part in my life by teaching me the value of a dollar, what it took as a man to provide for your family, to have a personal relationship with the Lord, and to have a very strong work ethic. God Bless his soul as he was called home many years later due to an apparent heart attack.

We ended up going inside and taking a seat next to one of the Great Danes that was now becoming older, lazy and would take up half the entryway stretching those long legs. As we joined hands together throughout the home and bowed our heads, Reuben was instructed to lead the prayer, and I tell you what! This kid was truly advanced in that area. That had to be the greatest, young, preteen biblical scholar I had known personally growing up.

After the two-hour-long Bible study, Rodney and I were out the door, and on to our next mission. In route to the 7-Eleven convenience store to stock up on supplies for our daily routine, I left the Bible study talking to God saying, “Lord, since you supplied your phone number, I can't help but call." Would I call? When would I call if I ever fully surrendered? What little did I know?

As we continued down past Camp Grill Bar, we opened the door to the mixed salt and pepper crowd inside and threw a pack of firecrackers Reuben had just sold us and ran all the way up towards Fifth Street laughing ecstatically.

Rodney and I then continued with our thirty-minute walk to the store. We eventually ended up at my Uncle Rickie's house with Antwan sitting on the front porch. Jokingly, Antwan asked Rodney for the canned soup and crackers he'd just stole from the 7-Eleven. He quickly replied, "No." And Antwan said, "Alright, chump," and put him in a WWE wrestling move, the sleeper hold, the Rick Flair signature move. Being that Rodney was sitting on the bottom step, Antwan was able to put him straight unconscious. Looking back over the years I think that did something to Rodney because when he woke up, he was a different human being.

Let the Games Begin

It's mid-October, Reuben's birthday and it's game time. We were on our way to our midget football game walking over an hour with equipment in our hands along a busy bustling highway, Route 837. We were headed to Duquesne High School football stadium that was near our ever so memorable Kennywood Amusement Park. It was a walk that we were all accustomed to making because we walked to Kennywood at least ten times a year. Once a year we all attended VIP style with new clothes, maybe new shoes, and a ride-all-day ticket. The other nine attendances were times we cleaned up as best we could, at least a few of us did, then headed across the bridge. One by one every 45 seconds one of us darted across the intersection and towards the entrance. However, we were already on the other side of the entrance behind the ticket gate and through the little hole, we had cut the fence that was covered by huge green bushes. Just that easy one at a time we were in. We were so good at it we even started getting on the rides without a ride-all-day pass or tickets. On our way back we'd stop at McDonald's across the street, eat, and hang out. The hanging out ceased one evening when a large crowd gathered and was freestyle battle rapping. Mc Honey and my cousin, Mike Stock, were rapping and some guy started rip rapping on them. Like a thunderbolt clap, Mike Stock had hit this guy and knocked him straight unconscious while he dropped hard to the asphalt. He laid there still, unconscious as everyone started fighting each other. A huge Homestead – Duquesne altercation ensued.

Once we finally arrived at our game that afternoon, Reuben finished with like 288 yards rushing and three fumbles. I picked up a new name during the game "The White Boy Express." We were playing Greenfield and these white boys were huge, or maybe I was just that small. I'll go with a combination of both. I was playing cornerback; the running back had just got the pitch and headed my way after he had just stiff-armed Crump. Just as he was almost past me, I lunged and hit him high. It felt like I didn't do much to his effect. as I was now holding onto one leg getting dragged for about 8 yards before taking him down. That day I heard, "The White Boy Express," all day long and for weeks and weeks after.

The following year things started to progress. I decided that would be my last year playing football I didn't feel like I'd be the next Ronnie Lott. What I did notice was that I was getting into girls a lot more, and an occasional bad decision.

I started noticing my mother was home much more after we moved again. We were eventually evicted from the apartment on Crawford Ave. and was now living on Hamilton street. We lived on one corner with a bar directly across from us. At the other end of the block were two more bars on each corner. One, in particular, was called Andy's. It was owned and operated by some middle-aged white guy. My Uncle Rickie's spot loafing with the other side as I took notice! His family, my cousins, had moved to the west side of Pittsburgh into another subsidized housing complex called Broadhead Manor. Rodney and I stopped hanging all the time but remained cordial towards one another. Due to the things Rodney was doing and always being on the go, I found it easier and more comfort in being with family learning and having fun. I at this point was chilling with Reub more and soon we came up with a plan that we were going to save our money and pitch in on a package.

Pitch in on a package? It won't be Christmas caroling anymore, I thought to myself no more Jingle Bells or Silent Night. No more having the white people turn their lights out and decorations off so we wouldn't knock on the doors. It's on Cuz. Rib Cookoff here we come!

We loaded up Daryl's vans and trailers with all the event goodies and supplies. We just smiled at each other as we set up the tables and carried the vending equipment. We worked so in sync and well together that when it came time to pay us Daryl was in the best mood I'd ever taken notice of. He blessed us two with $85 a day for the weekend event.

Chapter Four

You Gotta Get Ya Paper On

"911 is a Joke in Your Town," blasted from the green convertible mustang 5.0 with a white top. I take notice of the driver behind the wheel. Under the dark designer glasses was a brown-skinned guy. I took a harder glance and noticed it was Eric Taylor "ET" behind the wheel with a huge grin showing those itty-bitty small teeth. Just glowing and having every head turn as he zoomed by blasting Public Enemy from the speakers. Reub and I had just met Slicc and had got our now second flip. We grabbed an eight ball the first time for $350. We were now on the second one. It went so fast while we sat down the projects.

On this particular day, we decided we would sneak back out after Daryl went to bed. While down the projects selling our little things, Ms. Shirly came up and asked for a twenty. I give her the twenty, she went and smoked it, and then comes back demanding her twenty dollars back with nothing that I gave her. This lady was annoying and very loud at times. You know, *that* lady. I went into defensive mode and the immature kid in me argues and gets loud with her. Her sister then comes outside along with her niece and made a scene that drew the attention of many. Soon after my sister came through with her friend. Before she could get out of the car, Shirly's family was up on the car talking trash to her about me. Dawn gets out of the car and a fight immediately ensued. My sister beat Niecey up so bad it was scary. She used her like a ragdoll. The respect for my sister after that was on another level by everyone. Word on the block was Dawn is a rumbler!

I hung out with all my little homies occasionally, particularly Slicc. He was always hanging around the Jets. I started being a bit rebellious at home after being told I was on punishment for missing days of school unexcused. With a constant itch to make more money, I didn't see a need for school. The pleasure that started to set in with being able to have what I wanted. I was becoming blinded to the real world. School wasn't fun anymore or even interesting. I started going to school for the first period then slipping out and going to the streets. I'd get put on punishment and climb out the window. Since my mother had started being home, she was more vocal and snappier on the spot about everything. I learned to turn into a graveyard shift worker.

One evening, I came into the house trying to go unnoticed as I went into my stash to 're-up'. I was on a money mission because my mom had signed off on me going on my first cruise. Slicc had asked if I wanted to go with his cousins Gadgey and Quick on a 5-day cruise. I was so excited to be going on an airplane and even more to be going on a cruise ship and different islands. This was my first trip and a trip that was a lot of firsts. My first vacation. I paid for it myself. My first vacation wasn't with my parents or siblings. My first vacation was with my new best friend, Slicc.

I was in and out of the house all evening trying to make sure I had my portion to contribute. Sure enough on my second trip back in the house, I could hear my mom arguing and fussing with Shank. "This is it. You're going to make some changes in your life, or I'm done. I've changed my life. I don't get high anymore. I go to the methadone clinic every morning and here you keep bringing this poison in my house every day. What you want me to do? Relapse and kill myself? You have 30 days. I'm giving you one month to clean up."

I just went about my business and sat on the porch, being it was getting late. Now I had an attitude thinking this guy wants my mom to be on drugs. *Oh really?*

Before long, Uncle Rickie walked up. "Nephew. Nephew, she got eighty." After that, I told Unc that he had to throw a rock at my side window if I didn't answer my pager. And sure enough, all night I was making money. My Uncle Rickie started using drugs and I was selling it to him. *What has gotten into me?* He hung out with the white ladies and our cousin, Harold, and the rest of the Steel Mill Boys. We called them that because after midnight they would all go to the mill and cut copper lines from the poles so that they could sell the copper at the scrap yard that opened at 5 am. Back then they would have crispy $100-dollar bills.

At times, we all became so dependent on it, that we would give them the poison ahead of time, partly because that meant they would come to us directly and spend their money because the competition was out all night.

Going to school became a nonfactor because I was up and out at all times of the night. There were nights, soon to be lots of nights, like that. After my mom bought a car, I'd sneak and take her keys and drift down the street before starting the car up. The only mistake was, I would return it with no gas and forget to put the seat back up. The first couple of times I got yelled at. Then as I started putting the seat back and filling up the tank, I almost didn't have to sneak anymore. Although the thrill I was getting from sneaking and riding from town to town was exciting. Yes, I taught myself to drive in the middle of the night practicing in my mother's car. I watched everyone drive and watched everything they did while I was riding as a passenger with them. Then I figured I'd apply it after hours.

One particular night, I had taken the car and was down the Jets on a late-night mission as we sat and shared a forty of Old English beer. Laughing, shooting dice, and hustling, the Mill Boys were asking for their 'wake up' before they headed down to go to work. Yes… work! Stealing copper was like their everyday hustle. Steal. Spend on drugs. Sleep all day. Get high all morning and night. As they soon made their way down to the mill, about two hours later, a bright light that lit up the sky appeared followed by sheer silence and darkness as all the lights in the two apartment buildings went dark. We then concluded that Daryl Woody, Harold or someone, one of the Mill Boys, must have cut the wrong line. And to our surprise we were right! A few minutes afterward, Daryl, Woody, Uncle Ricky and the rest of the crew appeared in a distance, dirty, wet, and dragging bolt cutters and thick-coated black and gray wire. "Clabo, come on man, give me a hit. I'm a nervous wreck. Harold just cut the wrong wire and electrocuted himself. Did you see the light in the sky? He's dead! He fell off the top of the pole! Please, Clabo give me a hit!"

I gave them all a hit and jumped in my mom's car and flew home. As I was exiting the car, adjusting the seat, and glancing at the near-empty tank with thoughts of, *oh boy, I gotta hear her mouth in the morning because I didn't put gas in it*. I thought quickly and went into my pocket and placed two $20-dollar bills on the seat before shutting and locking the door. Sirens could be heard a mile away. I laid still in my bed thinking, *wow my cousin's dad had just died.* That's my cousin. What is wrong with me? All I could think of was how to get the dollar. Was I becoming immune? Did the devil steal my soul?

The following day I woke up and paged Slicc. When he finally called me back, he informed me that he would pick me up after lunchtime in school and we would go out to the mall to shop for the trip. When he pulled up, I noticed there were two other guys in the car already. It was R-Dog and Butters. They quickly rearranged their seating and jumped in the back as I took the front passenger seat. As we're riding, we're discussing what needs to be done while we were on the trip. I told R-Dog I was leaving my pager and three bundles of work with him. These were one hundred packs. Three of them. Straight rocks. I then told him to give me $70 for each pack. He was just getting his feet wet for the first time, but it would be easy, I thought, since he would have my pager. We made it to the mall. We did more window shopping and getting girls numbers than anything else. We were soon back in Duquesne and just a mere wake up from going on my first vacation.

The vacation was nice, but what was more interesting was that a major conversation was taking place, and I was involved. I did more listening than anything. Gadgey moved to California and was working in a very important position for an airline. "I can get a whole one for ten thousand. The only issue is getting it there and getting the money back." "Well if you get it here, we can Western Union the money back. $4800 at a time." Enough said. It was now game time.

In a few hours, we'd be departing the ship. On the flight back home, Slicc asked how much I had saved up and if I was going to pitch in $2500. I told him that I only had $700 saved up and enough to buy another quarter ounce. After a few silent minutes of looking out the window at the clouds below, it hit me. "I got a plan, bro," I said in a whisper. "What's that? What's up?" he replied. "Shank, I'mma rob Shank!" "Shank who?" he retorted. "My mom's boyfriend. That old bastard. I'mma get him!" I said.

I then went on to explain that I had seen him with a lot of money one day and that he and my mom were arguing a little while back. As soon as we landed, we drove back to my house and nobody was home, and nobody knew I was home. I told Slicc to leave my bags in the trunk, park in the alley, and come on. As I'm walking toward my house, I realized that I didn't have my house keys. So, I checked under the mat as soon as we reached the porch. 'Yes! It's on!' I whispered in a still tone. As we entered, I directed him to watch out the front window while I ran upstairs to my mom's room. I darted up the stairs and was soon going through the drawers without uncovering anything. I turned to the side of the bed where he slept and still nothing. Nothing inside the nightstand. I looked underneath the mattress and under the bed, still nothing. I then went for the closet. As I was going through his gangster looking trench coats to my surprise, I felt a couple of huge bulges. I pulled out the items in the pocket and a bag full of colorful balloons sorted by color in a brown lunch bag was revealed. Then the inside pocket, I pulled out bundles of money wrapped in rubber bands, and in the other pocket a chrome snub nose 38 revolver with five bullets loaded in it. I screamed "Slicc! Jackpot! Yeah boy!" I ran down the steps pockets fully loaded and the brown bag in hand. I told him to hurry and grab a knife from the kitchen. When he came back into the dining room I said, "Cut the screen. Open the window and cut the screen." As he did that, I tossed around the sofa pillows and some papers that were on the table trying to make it look as if someone other than myself had burglarized my home. We left the window open and the door unlocked and ajar and was on our way to his house.

As we're driving, I'm counting. At the three thousand mark we pulled up at his house. I tucked everything back in as we went inside. The balloons became the topic of discussion because neither one of us knew what to do with it. Just as we're talking about it, this man with long dreadlocks comes walking down the steps. It was his father. He had just been released from prison for retail theft. The twenty-third one, and not the last either.

We tried to hurry and throw a pillow over everything, but his eyes were quicker than our hands. He asked, "Why ya'll hiding something? I know ya'll bad asses selling coke. The whole damn city knows! And whatever you two got, I want some right now!"

After a few words, we asked him, "Well, what's this?" His eyes opened wide as he said, "That's the dope that's in the city. They sell that on the Hill. That's the raw dope. Hold on. Give me two. Let me see." As soon as we gave him a couple, one blue balloon, one yellow balloon, he said, "Hold on. I'll be right back." Maybe ten minutes later he was back. He was scratching and rubbing his hand and his arms saying, "Yeah, that's it. You got something there, son. That's a 10!" "A 10?" I chimed in, "What's a 10?" He replied, "That's better than the bags that Hicks has. It's number one now!"

Now I had heroin and plenty of it. A gun. Coke. And close to four thousand dollars. Not counting what R-Dog had for me or the $700 that I had saved up but forgot to grab when I robbed my home. Slicc talked me into putting the whole $4000 up while he only put a thousand of his own money up. We were ready, though. We had our $5000 total that he needed. My mom blew my pager up and contacted everyone in the neighborhood and also rode around. She even made her way to Slicc's house and demanded to be let inside.

After a couple of days, I was on the block up the Heights and my mom rolled up on me from behind in her Ford LTD. With the look of fury and pain in her eyes, her voice raspy and crackling, she sobbed, "Why would you do this to me? Why? Do you know that Shank thinks you robbed him, and he says he's going to find you?" I turned and looked her dead in the eyes and said, "Yes, I did it. I'm sorry. But tell him I'm around. I'm always around. And I got his pistol, too. And if he sends another threat, I'll be to see him." She went on to say he doesn't have anything now and he's flat broke. I then told her that I would give some of the balloons back, but that I wasn't putting it in her hands and that I would have Uncle Rickie give it to him. That never transpired and before I knew it, he had packed up and moved out. I was so grateful and happy that it happened the way it did.

Chapter Five

I Had to Get Ya

Mom was now going to church regularly, even Bible studies on weeknights. My sister was pregnant with her first child and still going to school as well as working evenings. The streets were becoming more and more relevant and so was I. My clothing was now fresh when I wanted it to be. I still had the hustler's ambition though and would sometimes be a Viking and wear the same clothes for a couple of days, take a shower and change my underclothes and go. I rarely got dressed to go stand on a corner and run to cars as they pulled up. I never understood that mentality of some of the hustlers. I guess I'd someday understand or maybe not. Not only was I one of the youngest dealers in town, but I was also carrying a gun every day and being the young immature kid that I was, I would sometimes let it be known I had one on me. I was still quiet and observant, but now I would also pull on you if I felt the urge to do so. We were now starting to roll. Our first package arrived and not before long the second and third. Slicc decided he wanted to hurry up and flip because of the pressure he was getting from his cousins to do so. He started chasing the cash instead of allowing the cash to chase him. He started fronting the product to too many different people, which I wasn't in agreement with. He wasn't a confrontational person nor someone who wanted to fight or anything. So some people were aware and would take full advantage of that and would not square up with him. A lot of guys were jealous also because he was driving a BMW, had money for lunch in school, and all the little girls were after him. On the other hand, I was straight thuggin'. We started traveling more to house parties around town and in other neighborhoods. He had family on his dad's side in Clairton they were our high school's sports rivals. Occasionally, we would go over and see them, to talk about any and everything. We loved to go to the local pool hall to eyeball all the girls…'cause they always liked the 'Duke Boys'. Most of their guys hated that! I stayed selling small pieces to the locals. I broke all my packages down. My older cousin Tina Garth was an addict that lived in Burn Heights and she was probably the biggest spender in Duquesne. She knew all the white folks. She must have gone to school with them. On this particular evening, she had a black lady with her that was very attractive, dressed well, and had the look of a new crackhead. This lady went by the name of Terri. Terri was spending crispy one hundred dollar bills several times a day with multiple dealers. Tina Garth called me to her little yellow pinto. "Hey cuz. Come here. Are you working?" to which I quickly replied, "Hell yeah," and ran to her car. She told me she wanted a 'teener'. A teener was one point seven grams. From my pocket, I pulled out several individually wrapped pieces and handed them to her. In exchange, she put one hundred forty dollars in my hand.

The following day, Slicc came to me and said that he was having a problem with some kid named AK in another town who owed him money but didn't want to pay up. He said AK was giving him a hard time, so we decided it was time to take a trip over to McKeesport where he lived. It was me, Slicc, his cousin Shades, and G-Fight. Shades ended up driving his car so that we could be a little more incognito. After fifteen minutes of driving up and down the streets of McKeesport, I spotted a guy walking a Pitbull puppy as I was peering out the rear window of the Buick Regal. I yelled, "Yo, that's him walking down that side street. Back up!" Shades whipped the car back with a quick jerk and made a screeching right turn onto the side street. I could smell the rubber from the tires burning. I was in the backseat with G-Fight as he growled, "Bro, let me get him. Let me out. Stop the car." Shades and Slicc had to get out first so that G-Fight and I could hop out from the back. Shades pulled up and we pushed the front seats in a hurry to rush them up out of the car. Slicc yelled out to AK, "What's up man? You got that?" AK snarked back, "I told you earlier what was up." His walk turned into a slight jog as he attempted to retreat, but he wasn't getting off that easy. Ole boy pulled out the .38 snub and squeezed without so much as a blink. BOOM! One single shot from thirty yards away and AK dropped right where he stood. We all scrambled to get back in the car, but not G-Fight. He ran up on AK and ran his pockets. He took everything out. We shouted frantically for him to come on and get in the car, but he was busy chasing the defenseless man's puppy. Soon to be his new puppy. He finally caught him by stepping on the leash, nearly snapping the puppy's neck in doing so. He scooped the puppy into his arms and ran towards the car. Police sirens blared from every direction as they drew closer to the scene. Shades drove us away as if nothing happened. He obeyed all of the traffic signs and signals to keep suspicion off of us. Meanwhile, he was pitching a whole fit about G-Fight having a puppy in his car. G-Fight laughed and played with his new puppy the whole ride back. He called him Fido. I was quiet and thinking in my head the whole ride back until Slicc started whining, complaining, and crying asking why we had to do that and demanding that we split up as soon as we hit our city limits. I retorted, "Ain't nobody splitting up. We came together. We're going back together. And we're staying together the rest of the night." I then directed Shades to drive the back way to the woods so that we could hide the gun and get rid of the shell and remaining rounds. He complied and soon pulled up behind the back steps of the projects. I jumped out of the car and ran deep into the woods. I was so far ahead that no one could even follow me. Deep in the thick of it, I crawled on my hands and knees and found a spot to dig. I flung leaves, sticks and dirt every which way as I unearthed a hole deep enough to bury the pistol.

First, I emptied the shell and the other four rounds, then I wrapped everything in my t-shirt and dropped it all in the pit. I scooped and pounded the dirt down on it and hand shoveled debris back on top to make it inconspicuous. Just then a rabid raccoon scurried toward me and began pacing in circles as white foam dangled from its' mouth. I needed to get out of dodge, but I needed to mark that spot. I grabbed a faded Pepsi can and tossed it near the hole just in case I needed to come back one day and retrieve it. I was almost out of the woods and from that distance, much to my dismay, I could see my boys being shook down by the police. They each had their hands up against Shade's car. My eyes darted from them to the unmarked police car with no visible overhead lights that were pulled up behind them, to the white men in uniform with their backs to me. I slowly eased back into the covering of the trees and switched my pager to vibrate. From the shadows of the woods I watched. The two police officers patted each of my boys down and then searched the car from hood to trunk. They came up empty-handed except for a nickel bag of funk that G-Fight had left in the ashtray. The officers questioned them about their presence there, even though they were just sitting. They instructed them to leave because one of the neighbors noticed them sitting in the car and felt it was suspicious enough to call and report. They had run Shades license and after everything came back clear, they jumped into their cruiser and pulled off. As I crept from the cover of the wooded darkness, I could hear G-Fight explaining that he always wears shorts underneath so they can't feel what he has. I was nervous, sweaty, dirty, and stinky. Shades was the first to see me. "Naw man. You can't get in the car like that," he exclaimed. "Alright, man," I replied. "Just pop the trunk and I'll put my pants in there. Then take me home so I can change really quick." He opened the trunk and got in the car. I took my pants off and put them in the trunk as promised and then headed to the passenger door. It wouldn't budge. These dudes had locked the doors and were laughing hysterically as they slowly pulled away. "Alright. Play if you want to. When I catch you, I'mma do you next," I warned. "Better yet, I'mma bust all your windows out the next time I see you." Baffled, Shades sneered, "Dang, man! You always talking crazy! Chill out and get 'cha butt in!"

The joke was over, and all the laughing ceased, but I was still annoyed. I forcefully slammed the front seat forward, thrusting Slicc into the dashboard to make room for me to climb in the backseat. We drove off with G-Fight stuttering over a laugh "Cuz, you crazy!" Yeah, crazy is exactly how I felt sitting in a car with three other young men wearing only a t-shirt, some tighty-whities, and basketball socks!

Shades soon pulled up in front of my mom's house and waited while I ran in to throw on some sweatpants. As I headed back out of the house, I glanced at the blurry TV screen showcasing the news and stopped dead in my tracks with my mouth ajar. "What just happened?" I exclaimed. But there was no answer I looked around. Nobody answered because nobody was there. "Is my mind playing tricks on me?" I was alone and talking to myself. *I must be losing it* I thought to myself. I mean, it was normal in our house for the TV to be left on when no one was there. My mom preferred it that way. She said it will give the appearance of someone being home to anyone on the outside peering in. I focused in on the news report as I reached for the dial on the 19-inch tube to turn up the volume.

"Breaking news when we return," stated the broadcaster. "Yooooooooo… COME HERE!!! HURRY UP Y'ALL!!!" I yelled out the screen door I'd flung open. They all came running. "Sit down," I stammered. "The news is about to show it!" Slicc started crying. "Man, we going to jail for life. YOU KILLED HIM!"

"Breaking news. Live from McKeesport, we are on the scene of an active investigation where a shooting occurred a short time ago. We have one young man that was shot in the back and robbery appears to be the motive. His injuries are life-threatening. The victim is conscious but refusing to talk. As you can see from this footage, the victim has lost a lot of blood. He was taken to McKeesport hospital for emergency surgery. No further information is available at this time. Live from the scene…"

The words faded and the room fell silent. Nobody moved. Nobody said a word. I reached for the dial and turned the volume back down. We filed out of the house one by one, dazed and consumed with our thoughts of what was to come. Back in the safety of the shade (Shade's Buick Regal), I broke the silence. "Look. The news said he isn't talking to the police. Yeah, his injuries are life-threatening, but he's alive. He's gonna make it." I directed my gaze to Slicc. "Although he only knows you Slicc, it's cool. We're good. So quit all that crying. Scary boy."

We rode through the streets headed nowhere in particular. Somehow, we ended up at Mr. Buddy's pool room on South Second Street. We were there long enough to walk through and play a few games of Pac Man while the old-timers played poker or tonk in the back room. Mont and ET were playing pool. Little kids were hanging around just enjoying the atmosphere. Their hands were full of quarters for the video games, Swedish fish and Sugar daddies. There was a good vibe. No drama was in the air. Everyone was getting along.

We soon headed back out, throwing up a few nods out of respect as we departed. Everything seemed normal and felt like it was back to the grind. We were nearly back to the car when out from between the dilapidated buildings a masked man appeared wielding a small machine gun, a tech nine to be exact. He seemed to be after Slicc as he called out his name as he approached us. "Slicc. What up now. You real tough on the phone talking to my girl, right." By this time, we all recognized the voice and knew what this situation was about.

The week before, Slicc had stepped to this dude's girl and gotten her number. They'd been conversing on the phone into the wee hours of the morning. One night, Trot snatched the phone from her and had words with Slicc. Trot and Slicc were always at odds. Trot was jealous. He and Slicc always went after the same girls. Always! Trot struck fear into many because he had a bad reputation and was known to be ruthless and sneaky. He was a 'stick up boy'. He would rob anyone. And not just rob them, he'd shoot them, too. And when he wasn't threatening with a gun, he was menacing the locals with his two pit bulls. He would act like he was going to turn them loose on people or make them bite.

On this night, he was his usual suspect self in full out stick up boy mode. He made Slicc empty his pockets and took every red cent he had. He got him for his watch, his stopwatch, and his gold chain that had the Mercedes charm on it. After he took his valuables, he took his pride. He open hand smacked Slicc in the face and told us to "get the f**k out of here!" We made haste. Shades started up the car and we were out! In the safety of the shade, I told Slicc that what Trot did was unacceptable and that he had to do something about it, or I would. I told him that he had to man up or everyone was going to try him and keep coming at him from every way possible. Slicc didn't say anything. He just gazed out the window and blew spit bubbles. At that moment I regretted having stashed the .38 snub in the woods. I certainly would have used it. My heart was pumping at a wicked rapid pace. I growled, "I ain't the darn one!"

Days passed and we came upon another pistol. G-Fight bought a 9mm from some Caucasian crackhead that drove a new teal Volvo. Somedays his Volvo would be our 'rent-a-rock'. We'd drop him off at his house and he would let us joy ride. We'd have the car back around 5:30 am just before his wife got home from work around 7 am. She was an emergency room nurse that worked the graveyard shift. She had no idea that her husband was smoking crack and loaning their brand-new Volvo out in exchange for a crack rock. Hence the term 'rent-a-rock'. He even told us he'd buy us guns from the store and later say they were stolen. It was on and poppin' now. We were armed with multiple pistols and ready for whatever. Ready to bring it by any means necessary.

I had gone back into the woods to retrieve the 38 snub the day after my homie Slicc got robbed and roughed up. Not only did I have it on me at all times, but I spent the time to sharpen the bullets… just in case. What happened the other day in front of the pool hall had me shook. I mean, I had just buried it for fear of what else could happen after the dude from McKeesport got popped and then WHAM! We're on the receiving end of the barrel. From that moment forward, I promised myself that I would never get caught slipping like that again. I told myself and my boys that I'd rather get caught up with it than to be caught without it.

This One's for You

We sat on my Grandma Evelyn's porch laughing and talking. Periodically, I'd go in and check on her and ask if she was alright or if she needed anything. She'd be laying on the couch with a glass of gin sitting on the old rickety wooden table. On the floor sat her go-to gallon. Grandma Evelyn, Gram as I lovingly called her, was my favorite. Not a day passed that I didn't check on my grandmother. She lived on 4th Street now and the school was about a mile up the road. So, everybody walked past my Gram's on their way home from school. 4th Street ran adjacent with Priscilla Avenue or 'PA' as it came to be known so Swamps, the local corner store, numbers joint, and the gambling spot, was two doors down from Gram's.

Butters and R-Dog were sitting on the porch, and I was sitting on the bottom step of the porch, all of which had the wood covered over with fake green grass carpeting. We watched G-Fight as he moseyed from the corner of Swamps back to Gram's with his new puppy in tow. We were all supposed to be in school, but for us, the class was being held in my Gram's backyard or on her front porch. We'd leave after lunch the days we did go to school and pretty soon my grades became flag poles. I sat on the bottom step scraping bullets back and forth on the sidewalk to sharpen them. My goal was to make them as sharp as AK bullets and call them the 38Ks. That way if Trot ran up to us again, I was going to blast him right through his coat.

Speaking of coats, I was wearing my tan Carhart coat with the two big chest pockets. I could fit my gun and my hand in at the same time without it even looking like I had anything. Within a few hours, I had three bullets completely shaved and sharp as ever. They were so sharp that if I even barely poked someone with one of them, they would bleed. *Am I looking for death around the corner? Is that what I see? Would anyone care if I died?* All manners of wicked thoughts chased each other in my mind over the next few days. Only now, I was ready to act on them. All of my bullets were new-needle-sharp. The 38K was ready for action. It would demolish anything in its path. And I was ready and willing to pull and make it happen.

Over the next few weeks, I built a reputation to let everyone know that I was not the one to play with. Just as Trot had earned a reputation down on 2nd Street and around the way that he wasn't to be taken lightly (and had a gang of young kids that idolized him to prove it), I was doing the same. I had all my friends following my lead and doing what I thought we should do. Subconsciously, I was waiting for our next encounter with Trot. In my mind, I could see him laughing to himself and saying, 'I had to get ya!' after humiliating Slicc.

This Is Deep

I hustled hard and hung out with my friends every day. I had no problems with anyone in my neighborhood unless I created them. Most of the kids around my way were former teammates anyway so I was good with everybody. One evening I decided to head to Burns Heights to hang out with Darryl and Dre. They were cousins and Dre's stuttering foolish self was always into something. He was the opposite of his older brother, TB, who was pretty laid back for the most part. Sometimes he would put us up to what he called a 'challenge' and that usually resulted in him having to fight because Dre was bothering someone or doing something that he had no business. Tonight's business was a robbing spree. Darryl, Dre, and I walked from Burns Heights through every inch of town with our final destination being just outside the Jets. About halfway there, we stopped and robbed two guys on South 2nd Street. It was easy. Somewhere along the way, Dre stammered out, "Clabo, let me hold the gun, man. Let me get 'em this time." I didn't think much of it as I handed him the gun. I'll never forget the vivid sound of the hammer cocking back and the words, "Break ya-self boyyyy," fight to escape from his mouth. Again, he stuttered "b-b-b-break yay a ya-selfffffff boyyyyy. I-I-I-I'm ssss-ssss-serious. Empty everything out 'cho pockets." I could hear myself inhale and exhale as I felt the cold steel of the snubbed barrel against my temple. He was shuddering and his shaky finger just a hairpin away from the trigger. That 38K would launch one straight into my brains. *What just happened.* Just that fast the tables had turned, and I was once again defenseless and in a bad situation. *Was I being taught a lesson? Was God about to take my pain away so suddenly by calling the end forward now? Or was this karma?* I suddenly felt my legs go weak as I dropped straight to the ground. I must have peed myself a little on the way down because the boxers I wore under my Cross-Coloured jeans were wet. "Empty ya pockets before I blast you ni**a!" Darn it! He had my gun. My gun! My 38K. My 38K that was loaded with bullets that I'd spent hours sharpening to ensure that they would glide through any Teflon bulletproof vest that was on the market. I went into my pockets and emptied everything. Dre motioned to Darryl to get the goods. His voice shook in unison with his finger that was near the hairpin trigger. My fear was at an all-time high. I braced myself, but they took off running. I finally made it back on my feet still weak in the knees though. I yelled out behind them “Alright! I’mma see you boyyyy! Believe that! I’ll see you again!” They were at the bottom of the hill by then. I limped off confused, shaken, and angry. It happened again. My body writhed with fury. I had to step my game up big time!

Chapter Six

Thank God for Small Favors

I woke up one morning and decided to see what was happening at school. I would show up periodically to catch up with who I could and to check out the girls. Most of the time when I went to school, I carried but this particular day I didn't. It was me, Rodney, and Sweetpea walking together this morning. Tina M. and some of her friends walked behind us giggling and being flirty. We were at the intersection and we noticed a Duquesne police cruiser approaching; they are riding very slow. We stood still, making sure not to walk out in front of them. Together, we motioned for them to continue past us and then we would cross. Instead, the car screeched to an abrupt halt and the officer jumped out. He barked that we come over to where he was, and the fellas and I complied. Next thing I know, he's yelling, "Turn around and put your hands behind your back. You have the right to remain silent." I hung my head in defeat and didn't utter a word. *We didn't even do anything.* I finally found the courage and asked, "What the heck am I being arrested for?" To which the cop retorted, "You'll see soon. You're going to jail for a long-time buddy." "I am not your freaking buddy and I didn't even do anything," I snapped back. He slapped the cuffs on me and shoved me in the back of the patrol car. He didn't even search me. I had $100 worth of crack on me and just enough time to maneuver that plastic baggie out of my pocket and stuff it down between the seat before we arrived at the police station. Thank God for small favors! We exited the patrol car and I hear him say, "We got one more." "Oh snap! They got Clabo, too! They got that young boy. That's messed up!" "Got me for what?" I held my breath. "Terry Lewis young buck. That chick Tina Garth had spending that change. You must have sold something to her young buck." "Oh." I sighed with relief. *I thought I was being arrested for what took place with the shooting a couple of weeks ago.* "We are all going downtown though. You, you're going to Shuman Center young buck for at least 10 days." *Shuman Center!* I thought to myself.

I was fingerprinted, my mugshot was taken, and thrown into a cell. *I'm only 13 years old. I shouldn't be here! What has happened? Would I straighten up? Where was my life headed? What would my mom say?* We rode past the school on the way to the police station as I gazed out the window thinking that school would be such a safe place to be today. Not long after, the cell door clanged behind me for the first time, I heard jingling keys drawing nearer. Soon I could see the keys. They were on this huge keyring in the officer's hand. "Mr. Clabo place your hands behind your back and face the wall with your arms extended," he stated very matter of fact. I didn't put up any gruff and just did as I was told. I was cuffed and escorted out of the cell, out of the building, back into the back seat of a patrol car and off again. I will always remember that ride. It seemed it was the longest ride ever. "Young man, you'll be going away for a long time. I hope you're ready because there are some tough young men where you're going." I didn't say a word. I just ignored him; well I tried to anyway. I looked up and started counting the stoplights. In my mind, I assured myself that whatever happened I was ready. Besides, I might just run into my friend who was arrested a couple of days before for stealing a car. Soon, the traffic lights were gone and the road on which we traveled looked as if it led to a castle. The road was lined with trees and freshly groomed shrubbery. Peering off into the distance, I could see a building that didn't quite look like the jail I had imagined. It wasn't a tall building. It was only one-story high. And there was no barb wire fence around it. The brick building was red and clean. The officer pulled up to a gated entry point, rolled down his window, and pressed the red button on the intercom. "Sergeant Slaughter here. How can I help you?" said the voice coming through the intercom's speaker. "This is Lieutenant Addams from the Duquesne Police Department. We have one in custody," said my driver. "10-4," Sgt. Slaughter replied. 10-4? What the heck is 10-4? Stoically, I continued to take in my surroundings. Soon the black gate at the point of entry to the back of the clean red brick building slowly crept open. I had butterflies in my stomach now. Things had just gotten real. The patrol car pulled forward to the guard who directed him to park in space 4. The officer got out of the unit and opened the back door to get me out as well. He told me to stand still and don't move. Through the back door, he leaned into the car and yanked on the seat. The whole back seat lifted out. *Wow! I've never seen anything like that before!* Thank God for Small Favors. If this was the original officer who arrested me and the original police cruiser in which I was detained, I'd be facing more charges.

As it was, I was being charged with delivering a controlled substance. He finished whatever he was doing back there and popped his big head back out of the cruiser. He slammed the door with one hand and pulled and pushed me in front of him with a single motion with the other. "Right this way," said the guard who was stationed at that checkpoint signaling with his huge arms for us to follow him. We were led into the building with the clean, red, brick exterior. The officer from Duquesne PD slid some paperwork underneath a glass window to the curly-haired old white lady that sat on the other side of it. She slid something back to him and he signed. She grinned at him and wished him well as he turned to depart. He exited through the iron door and it clanked close with a loud thud. He was on the outside and I was on the inside.

"ON THE LINE!!!" He barked, "Don't look anywhere except straight ahead. Follow me." *Who in the h*ll is he talking to? I bet if we were outside of here, he wouldn't be talking crazy like this.* I glanced around me to see if anyone else was offended like I was, and things became grim and reality set in. I wasn't in the streets. I was now in the custody of an Allegheny County juvenile detention facility and unsure about what lay ahead of me. We entered a room that had a cubicle about chest high with brick surrounding an eight by eight area. I was instructed to take off my belt, untie my shoelaces, and strip down. So, I took off everything except my underwear and t-shirt. He frowned at me as his eyebrows nearly met his hairline. "I said strip down. Can you understand English kid? I mean everything." He scowled and stretched his eyes as if to say 'duuuuuuuhhhhhhh'. "Oh okay," I replied, humiliation setting in. I hesitantly complied. "Now turn around, drop, and squat. Turn back around, grab your crotch, and cough two times. Open your mouth. Tongue out." This was awful. I was completely humiliated. He then gave me a stained towel, a dingy washcloth, a pair of striped pants, a shirt, a pair of underwear, and a pair of socks. I had to trade my Timberland boots for a pair of BoBo's. I showered, got dressed, and signed the inventory sheet with my personal effects listed in detail. The next stop was a holding cell already occupied by four other individuals.

I wasn't there long before a female guard with a cart stopped in front of our temporary quarters. She had with her a helper of sorts. The guard pulled out her keys, opened our door, and called out, "Line-up!" Everyone jumped up, stood in a straight line, and got quiet. "Here is lunch," she informed us, and her assistant handed each of us a brown paper bag. I took my bag and peered into it while I sat down. "A cheese sandwich," one of the other kids huffed and moaned. I pulled my sandwich from the bag in disbelief and it sure was. It was a thick slice of yellow American cheese between two slices of wheat bread. Further down in the bag was an apple, a pack of peanut butter crackers, and a small carton of skim milk. I took the apple out and bit into it. Then took another bite and another. With a mouthful, I offered up the remainder of the bag's contents. "Anybody want this?" I said between smacks. Some kid from the East Side mumbled something inaudible followed by a mischievous grin and no good chuckle that I'd heard many times being in the streets. "COUNT TIME!" blared from the speakers that were inset into the walls and the forceful rap of the guard's keys against the window jarred us from the light moment we were having. "STAND UP!" he screamed at us as we had all fallen into a still and silent state of staring. We jumped to our feet and stood waiting until we heard "count cleared" announced over the speaker. "Coffee. Clabo. Taylor. Henley. Let's go." We formed a single file line and stood to wait for the next command. I asked the guard when we would get to make phone calls. "You might get a call today if your counselor is on the block. He will give you one emergency call within the first 24 hours of your being in custody," was his reply. I thanked him and we marched forward through system-controlled doors and various checkpoints. We stopped after marching for about three minutes and the guard announced "Coffee. Clabo. This is your stop." We hit the unit and a hush fell over the room. Each one of the 62 young men already in there stopped and stared at us. Some of them were in the middle of card games; some of them were gathered around the TV, and some of them were gathered in small groups chatting it up. They stopped and they stared. Out of nowhere, Coffee dropped his newly assigned belongings, sheets and all, and growled, "If anybody wanna do something let's do it now!" He stared defiantly at each group waiting for someone to accept his challenge. "That's what the heck I thought," he hissed. He picked up everything he'd thrown down and stomped toward the booth that was in the middle of the unit. "Room 207 top bunk," the guard said to me. "Coffee. 209. Bottom." I went straight to that cell and sat my belongings on the bed. My cellmate was in there already sitting at the desk drawing a picture of a picture. He turned around and said, "What up, bro. Were you in the car with Marcus?" "Marcus who?" I asked. "Yo, you just came in with Coffee. That boy was just on the news. He did a drive-by and killed a few people on Penn Ave. He's a nut. He's into that gang banging, bro." Neither one of us said anything more.

I walked out into the common area in search of the counselor, so I could get my phone call, only to find that he was already gone for the day - no phone call. Irritation was swelling and settling in my soul. *No phone call; nobody knows I'm here, and I'm locked up with a bunch of knuckleheads. Was I a knucklehead too and just couldn't see it in myself?* I grabbed a seat near the tv and watched with the intent of seeing what was on the news. "My man, yo, that's my seat," said a kid about my height with 35 pounds plus my weight who intentionally stood directly in front of me obstructing my view of the TV. I didn't put up a huff. I got up without saying a word and walked behind everyone seated around the TV. I could hear their sneers and the chuckles as I passed. I grabbed a plastic chair from an empty table nearby and calmly walked back to the TV area. I stood there with my chair. Nobody paid me any attention as they were all tuned in to the breaking news, so I sat down and joined them. Coffee's name and face were splashed on the screen as the news reporter stated that he was accused of killing three men with an assault rifle and had been arrested not far from the scene. The news report went off and someone changed the channel. I stood up, picked the chair up and raised it as high as I could above my head, and then with every bit of rage and force I felt following through me, I smashed it down on the guy's head who tried to punk me. I yelled, "Here's your seat. Sit here. Here's your seat!" with every blow I delivered. Within moments I was being restrained and removed from the unit. Hopefully, my message was received. That it is not the size of the man, but the size of the heart and the fight inside the man that matters. Hopefully, Fat Boy learned that lesson and we didn't have to have that conversation again.

Here I am getting myself into more trouble. I was carted off to isolation and stripped of everything. A guard told me that I would be moved to another unit again after shift change because they had watched the tape and noticed that Fat Boy was trying to bully me. He went on to say that I would be there at least ten days before my hearing. Then on the day of the hearing, the judge would do one of two things: recommend that I remain incarcerated for an additional 30 days or deliver my sentence if the state was prepared to proceed with the evidence.

Those were ten of the longest days of my life. The same routine day in and day out. The monotony of it all was abysmal. I was so excited when day ten finally rolled around. I jumped up when the cell doors sprung open for breakfast call and court. My attorney had come to see me the night before but couldn't give me any clear answers. He only said that he thought I'd be alright. Before long, those of us headed to the court that day were loaded into a van and on our way. Once we arrived, we were placed in what they called a holding tank. The name was no misnomer and was appropriate being that there were sharks and piranhas, and even a few goldfish amongst us. One by one an Allegheny County sheriff called each of our names and escorted us to court individually. I watched as a few came back with smiles happy that they'd gotten probation. The vast majority of them were white boys. There was one black kid amongst them. He and a white kid had committed a robbery, so he was sentenced lightly like the white kid. I was optimistic. I thought for sure things would go well for me, also. That is until Coffee came back and said that he got juvenile life. Looking back on it, that was pretty light considering that he had taken three innocent lives. He was 13 when it happened so juvenile life meant that he would serve five years in juvey and then be released when he was 18. *Is that the way this judicial system was designed? You kill your own and you get a short amount of time. Was I ready to follow that path? The road I was headed down didn't seem so too promising now!* "Clabo, you're up." I hopped to my feet and said a silent prayer. *"God please help me. If you help me, I won't be bad anymore." Was that a real prayer? Was I being sincere? Was it the whole truth or even partially true? Was I afraid of the unknown and looking for a way out?* From the elevator and into Judge Williams' courtroom I went. I saw my mother, my sister, and my friend, Slicc. They stood behind me toward the rear of the courtroom. All I could do was nod my head as a greeting and acknowledgment. I turned forward towards the judge's bench, but she was not yet seated. Then the sheriff said, "All rise. The Honorable Judge Williams' court is now in session," as the judge appeared out of her chambers through a door that blended seamlessly with the oak wall and wooden trim. An African American Woman as a Judge. Interesting. Her eyes held captive the fire of Hestia and a flame was thrown my way as she briefly glanced at me before giving everyone the, "please be seated," directive. Nervously, I sat fumbling my fingers together. I kept my eyes on her and forced myself to concentrate and listen as closely as possible.

Judge Williams was looking down at the paperwork in front of her. She looked up and said to me, "Young man, do you realize the gravity of the charges you face?" To which I responded, "Yes ma'am." She said, "Do you realize that I can send you to Vision Quest for two years?" I was shocked and remained silent. She continued speaking. *Vision Quest? Two years? Wait...what?* So much for concentrating and listening intently. I looked to my right at my attorney when I heard him state, "Yes Your Honor." *Yes, what?* I had no idea what was said nor what had just happened. *What did he just agree to?* We made eye contact. The look on my face must have said dazed and confused because he leaned over and whispered to me that she had just sentenced me to 6-months at the Allegheny Academy.

Allegheny Academy? That big blue van? I muttered an okay and looked back at my mom. My attorney and the prosecutor approached the judge's bench and after a brief sidebar, she pounded her gavel. Handcuffs were placed on my wrists again and I was led out of the courtroom and back to the holding tank upstairs. My attorney was still by my side, so I asked him, "When am I getting out?" He said he didn't know, but that he would find out when he went downstairs to complete my paperwork. The sheriff chimed in. "You'll be gone today, son. Don't worry. It'll be about an hour." *Yessssssssss! Thank you, God! You came through! Yesssssssssss!!!*

Chapter Seven

I See Death Around the Corner

Here I am now in mid-November wearing a Karl Kani hoodie draped over my cornrows. walking home from school on my lunch break, and all of a sudden, I hear screams coming from everyone; followed by a BANG! with a loud echo that seemed to shake the whole city. I got home, opened the door and went straight for the kitchen. I poured me some Rice Krispy Cereal and covered them with milk. I listened as the Rice Krispies crackled in the plastic bowl. I hear a voice, "Clabo! Clabo! Let me in!" I turned toward the door and saw the panic on Rodney's face. He was frantic and rambling that he had messed up and just shot T-Bone in the stomach in front of everybody. He wanted to hide the gun in my house and camp out in my mom's basement where I had set up shop. "What the heck you do that for?" I screamed at him. "You're done, bro. He plays football and everybody loves him. He wasn't even thinking about you, bro." I'm really at a loss. "Yo, my mom will flip if she hears all of this and she sees you in her house! And I have to catch the van at 4:30 pm. You know I'm in the Academy now!" I told him to go on down there, but do not turn the TV on because she will look if she hears the television. I told him that he could stay down there overnight, but he had to go tomorrow. I headed out the door on my way back to school, but I was turned around because everything was roped off because of the shooting and the helicopter was there to life flight the victim with life-threatening injuries. And because the shooter was still at large. Imagine that. Police and news reporters from every station swarmed the place. This wasn't "fake news" as Trump likes to say. This was a real-life drama unfolding and impacting people's lives. News of the shooting was being broadcast live from the scene on every network and I was at home watching it; taking it all in. I'd been here at this exact moment before. My mind went back to when we rolled up on ol' boy from McKeesport and how a situation that I was so close to was being played out on TV. I was living it all over again. The anxiety, the paranoia, the FEAR! *Why does this keep happening?* I'm staring at the screen in a daze. Duquesne star running back, one of my childhood friends, was being carried to the helicopter waiting to transport him to Presby for a life-threatening gunshot wound; a gunshot wound that came at the hand of another childhood friend…who was sitting right next to me, petrified!

I See Death Around the Corner

My gaze shifted from the news to Rodney. He sat at the edge of the bed still hiding out in my mom's basement. Stress lines were spreading across his forehead and the fair-skinned chinky-eyed Korean looking dude looked mad worried. We had both just witnessed his picture being plastered on the TV screen as the newscasters identified him as the shooter and described him as armed and dangerous. They said a manhunt was underway. I let him know that later on that night after my mom was sound asleep that I would drive him to Broadhead down on the West Side so he could stay with my cousins, Rook and Antwan. Even though they had moved away, I still kept in touch with them and they would look out for me. He agreed. He said, "Yeah, I gotta go because I would shoot it out with them before I would go to jail. I'm not going to jail." But it was more than just the cops that he needed to worry about. Those Taylor's were a pretty large family and they had gained a lot of clout in the hood getting money. I heard a horn beep three times. It was the big blue van, my ride to the academy. I ran up to the screen door and signaled to the driver to give me a minute. I went to the academy every day from 4:30 pm to 8:30 pm and all day on the weekends for six months as mandated by the court. I had dinner there with the other kids in the program and we participated in a variety of skill-building activities. And we stood line a *lot* as a form of discipline. I was a young teenage boy and now a convicted felon. I was only thirteen years old and my journey with the judicial system had already begun. I was the product of my environment. *Was there any hope? Would God guide me and save me?* I prayed he would because I had made up in my mind that this would be my last day getting on that big blue van. I was going AWOL as they called it. I called it living on the run. Yep, by the time I got dropped off my mind was made up. I wanted to make more money. I'd be smarter this time. I knew exactly what and what not to do now. I'd heard so many stories; made so many new connects and had gained the respect. I was quiet, but I was known to be a head busser.

From my time at the academy, I'd watched and learned that you had to miss three consecutive days before they considered you AWOL and the hide and seek game began. So I knew I had a couple of day's head start to get gone. I had studied their actions and reactions down there. I wasn't the first to go on the run and I certainly wasn't going to be the last.

Things were heating up. I'm running wild like the wild child. Momma says, "Lord, please watch over my children," and prayed for me every night now, calling upon the Good Lord to keep his hands around me. My mother would tell me, "God had His hands on you from the jump, from the very beginning."

I got back that evening. Mom was upstairs resting already as she yelled downstairs "Clabo, is that you?" I replied with much respect and love, "Yes ma'am. Good night. I love you, Mom." "Alright. There are some hot dogs and cream corn on top of the stove. Put the food away when you're finished," she stated.

She didn't notice Rodney downstairs. Great! I ate quickly and went down into the basement to talk to him, but he wasn't there. I looked all around including in the bathroom; he was gone. On the bed lay a piece of cardboard that he had ripped off the box of Tide to leave a note. "Clabo, I had to go. Thank you for letting me stay. I love you like a brother. I will see you in a couple of days."

I looked under my bed pulled the saucer out of the bag and a safety pin, then went out the back door and lifted the grass in my secret spot and grabbed a quarter ounce. It was on tonight. I planned on staying up all night. I used the safety pin to break my package up into dimes and twenties. In a matter of minutes, I was done. I had cut my quarter up and put it into a medicine bottle. This evening it was an old Tylenol bottle that I had put fake grass around, just in case I had to throw it while getting away from the police. It would blend right with the natural grass and shrubbery. As I emptied my book bag and started stuffing it with clothes, my sister came walking down the stairs with her high school love, Chee. "What are you doing?" she whispered. "Nothing. Going out for a while. Page me if they call the house phone or if my PO comes here. I'm out, sis. I love you."

My mom had gotten a lot more vocal and stricter being that her addiction was in remission. That, however, still didn't stop me from drifting the car down the street in the wee hours after midnight. But it did make me more rebellious and hungrier. For what, though? Did I even know? I was sure on my way to find out.

Here we are going into 1990 and the era of "cars riding by with the booming system" and pagers being utilized by the neighborhood drug dealers. I waited for a while for my sister to go back upstairs then I tiptoed upstairs to see if she was asleep but to my surprise, she must have been checking on me first because all I heard was her and Chee making my soon to be nephew, D'Juan. I turned and eased back down to the kitchen, and as quietly as possible, lifted the keys off the table and then headed out. I drifted down to the stop sign at the bottom of the hill where two bustling bars were filled with drunks and hookers, as well as a pimp or two and plenty addicts. I turned the key and vroom vroom. I was out on my way down to the Jets to get a 40oz beer from Erie Pirl's apartment and hustle all night until the quarter ounce was gone.

Me, Slicc, Speedy John, and Clarkie G were taking turns all night. We hustled until the birds were chirping and when I did take the car back, this time I had a ride follow me because I was out. My mind was made up. It was time that I become my own provider, or so I thought.

Blind Leading the Blind

Slicc's mom loved me and was always so nice. Even after she cursed Slicc out first for something he'd done or didn't do, like the dishes or washing her car after he dropped her off at work. Yes, she allowed him to drop her off and WE had the car all day or evening, depending on what shift she worked that day. I somehow found myself living with Slicc while on the run, most of the time. Money was flowing. I made my first five thousand by myself while on the run. Probably smoked a good portion of it up on weed. Yes, I started smoking weed. The first time I felt like my worries went away as if I wasn't on the run anymore. When I smoked, it relaxed my mind from all the pain, worries, and anxieties I was facing as well as guilt because my mother was hurt. She tried to reach out and locate me after my PO, the Academy, and the Duquesne Police showed up at the house. Life on the run taught me a lot about myself. Good or bad, I would soon find out that you can run but can't hide for long. Your time will eventually run out.

Well, it eventually did run out, but not before I bought my first car, a tan Subaru hatchback station wagon. It was a manual transmission stick shift. It didn't have brakes, so I would break it down using the gears, which worked perfectly fine. Also, there was a hole in my floor underneath my mat, the double mat. In between those mats was the 357 magnum I had bought for eighty dollars of product.

Now, instead of going to school, I was driving past the school showing off and giving rides to the homies or young ladies. It was on now! I was on and I was getting noticed more. I barely slept due to the fact I was answering every page I got and all the trouble I was stirring up kept me on edge from retaliation and the police that was on me. They soon realized from either a confidential source or my stupidity that I was driving the Subaru and one evening those red and blue lights lit up behind me with the siren roaring. I without hesitation floored it and turned onto 3rd street flying through stop signs and hitting corners. I ended up with a police car still on my tail trying to hit my bumper to make me lose control. I decided I had to try and make it to Burns Heights so I could jump out and have the best chance of getting away. That's exactly how it turned out. I got to the top of the hill and hit the corner; never slowing down you could hear the tires as the rubber on the fifteen-inch steel rim scratched past the rental office. I jumped out with my 357 magnum in my hand and disappeared into thin air around one of the apartment buildings. Red and blue were everywhere and riding slow as I watched them from my cousin Tina Garth's window. They had no idea where I was, but they sure were all up in my car. Well, it technically was my car because I paid for it, however, I left the title in my customer's name.

Here I am on the run for a felony conviction that my cousin Tina unknowingly let happen. Now I'm holed up in her apartment with an issue regarding the law again. Within the hour a tow truck pulled up and off it went. As I was peeking out of the window, I noticed Dre and his cousin Daryl walking with a group of other kids. I waited until that last police car pulled off and then I dipped out the back door into the darkness around a building through the field and back by his cousin, Jerm Worm's apartment in the sticker bushes. I hid waiting for either all the crowd of kids to leave or move far enough away so I could get a clear shot on Dre. I really wanted him to walk off towards his apartment so I could run up on him and surprise him the same way he had shocked me, robbed me, and could've easily taken my life. I wanted my payback now as well as my pistol with the custom bullets I made. His older brother was even upset that he had done that to me. Big Nose TB was cool with me. We'd done a few things together in our early days. However, the thought of his feelings about what I wanted to do to his brother never crossed my mind.

I didn't seem to have any thoughts, feelings or remorse during this teenage period of my life. I was what I have enough sense now to stay away from, and respect to a degree. And that's a young ruthless kid with not one responsibility, care, worry, or fear in the world.

Maybe if I'd stayed playing baseball, I wouldn't be in this situation ready and willing to take a life that

God created so easily. Within the 53 minutes and 8 seconds that read on the stop clock that hung around my neck, I sat, and they stood and sat on the back porch. My pager started beeping just as the flashlight cops were hitting the corner. Smothering the pager with my hand, I used my index finger to switch it to off mode. The two beat--cops (security guards) glanced in my direction but continued walking and finished their rounds since they couldn't see anything. Once they were a distance away, I crawled out of the bushes and was off into the darkness. *I'd certainly catch up with him again.* But after wasting an hour waiting, it was time to get this money that was blowing up my pager.

Just outside the projects, I made my way to the payphone in front of the local tavern. This particular phone was known to be frequented by dealers, addicts, and thieves trying to retrieve the quarters, dimes, and nickels from inside. While I was standing there, VO was going into the bar saying he just *smashed 'em*. Smashed 'em was a term that hustlers used when they were sold out of everything they had for the day. "V can you get me a 40 of Old E, homie?" I asked. He grabbed my five dollars and came back out and said, "Here young buck and don't be gettin' it in and causing trouble. I saw you jump out of that car drawing all that heat out here." Life on the run started turning me into a menace.

One afternoon soon after, we were riding around just as school let out. I wasn't going to school, but as soon as school would let out, Slicc would come past Priscilla Ave near Swamps and I'd appear from between two houses and do what needed to be done and disappear back into the cut. I had my Gram's house, one of my old baseball teammates, Pin Head, was also living nearby, and as long as I had money, Swamp would allow me in, to gamble.

This particular afternoon, I jumped in as he was cruising around near the local Elks. I noticed CY walking and immediately told Slicc to slow down and stop. As he hit the brakes, the passenger door was already open. With the pistol in my hand, I ran up to a group of teenaged kids that had just got out from learning algebra and science, where I should have been also. Instead, I just pulled and had the pistol aimed point-blank range at CY. I was causing unnecessary trouble just because he was loafing with a couple of kids, I particularly didn't like much at the time. So I was going to punish him instead. "What's up. Empty ya pockets." He vaguely replied, "I don't have anything. I didn't do anything to you!" As he raised both his hands above his head in a protective way. I then got more aggressive and swung the pistol at him, hitting him repeatedly in the head. All of a sudden, the firearm discharged and let out a very loud cannon-like BOOOOOOMMMMM! He dropped straight to the ground in a fetal position. I turned and ran back towards the now getaway vehicle. *Had I just committed murder?*

What just had occurred without a thought or any real reasoning. I just took someone's child, brother, friend, and so much more. Now I'm on the run for this, also.

Praise the Lord CY didn't get shot in the head. He had dropped to the ground in fear just as I had when I faced the barrel with Dre. But once his mother found out, she pressed charges on me. Now I'm considered armed and dangerous along with the probation violation and being AWOL from the Academy. I was going to live my life like a thug 'til the day I died. And if I did die young, who cared?

On the run, I had so many spots I'd be dipping in and out of. Most of the time, I was with my homie Slicc, though. I had to grow up fast. The only way I thought I could survive was by taking mines and doing anything I had to do to eat. I'd gotten to the point where everyone stood clear of me. Older, younger, whoever. I demanded respect as I gave it in return to my elders. Just because you were an elder didn't quite mean you were respected, though. Because some elders were out to get you also and some were just flat out not to be respected simply being, they didn't respect themselves so why should I. Or so I thought back then. All my sister would say was, "Boy, you always into something." She was right because the street life is all I wanted to know. I felt like I woke up one day and screamed screw the world.

When I was coming up rough that wasn't even what you called it. I was smoking blunts and running with alcoholics, a car full of my homies when we rolled. Some days sippin' on Yac, I felt like I could see it in people's eyes they wanted us to fall off instead of ball. Then they'd wonder why I put the work in the way I did.

I caught a jitney, they call them Uber's now, down to my cousin's apartment on the west side of Pittsburgh. They drank, got money, gang banged and all over there. Everything went!

I'm sitting in the living room with my cousin Antwan, drinking a beer and pitching quarters against the kitchen wall when Rookie came running in the apartment saying, "Where's the freaking' gun, Twan? Where's the gun? I'mma kill this fool!" Twan was shook and said, "Man, I don't know." I started to pull mine and give it to him, but he ran off into the bedroom screaming, "I'mma kill this fool. He done threatened me!"

If anyone knew Rookie the way I did, then they knew he was serious about what he was saying. We went back to pitching quarters trying to get a John Harvey. Rookie flew back past the kitchen entryway and darted outside, leaving the door wide open. We ran to the door but didn't follow him as he ran down the concrete steps and across the street. We went back into the apartment and about thirty seconds later we heard a single shot.

BOOOOOOOMMMMM!!!

Screams and chaos ensued. By the time we made it to the bottom of the steps, Rook was slowly walking in our direction with the pistol in his hand. He walked up to us and said, “I gotta go. I just blew that boy’s head off.” *“What? Who? What the heck Rook? You killed ‘em?”* “Shut the heck up! Ain’t nobody gone threaten me and get away with it! Now let’s go. I’m going over the Duke for a couple of days then I’m going up the YO.”

We ran back into the apartment and started scrambling around. Tee ran in while all this was transpiring and asked, “Rook, what the hell you do?” Tee joked but halfway seriously asked, “You crazy, fool?” “Shut the hell up before I whoop ya butt Tee!” Rook snapped whipping his head around in Tee’s direction. “Shut up and come get these six ounces I got left. Here. I got fifty-five hundred. I’m taking that with me. Get rid of those Tee and see Diddy Dollars. He owes me for a half. Give him another one when he’s finished.”

Red and blue could now be seen and heard as a crowd had now gathered around another lifeless body. We dipped off in the other direction just, Rook and me.

I was told we were going to west gate to get a jitney back over my way. *Darn. I had just come over this way to hide and get away from the drama. Here I am getting deeper inside the game.* I didn't say anything though. *Cuz just killed somebody. I'm only on the run for minor things at least compared to what we were just living.* "Cuz, I'm not going to jail. I'll do whoever I got to!" Rookie said. "Cuz, I hear you. I'm with you, Cuz. I'm on the run too, Cuz," I replied.

By the time we made it back over to my way, we got dropped off at my mother's house, and not even thinking I just turned the doorknob and went in. "Boy what on God's green earth are you doing just walking up in here? You haven't been here in God knows how long and Rookie what are you doing?" "Hey Aunt Deb," he said in a soft, laughing voice as if he just came from church or something. We went on through the living room and down the steps. I hadn't even reached the bottom step when my mother screamed, "Boy get your butt up out of here! Rookie come here! What did you two just do? You're on the news. You just killed somebody. Shot somebody's head off at point-blank range." Rookie said, "Aunt Deb, he threatened me. I had to." My mom said, "Y'all gotta get outta here. Does your mother know what just happened? My God! Come here." She grabbed my cousin and wrapped her hands around him as tears streamed down her cheeks. She started calling on the Lord in prayer and asked God to "watch over these boys."

Afterward, she said, "Gone back downstairs and get some sleep and that's it. Tomorrow you both got to go!" I knew we weren't going to get off that easily and just be banished to the basement. We were down there for about fifteen minutes then my mother appeared and sat right next to us and lectured us both for what seemed to be infinity. For the first time, the thought crossed my mind, *darn even thugs worry.*

After the lecture, Mom rolled out. Rook and I started talking about the plan for when the sun came up the next day, being he was just on the news and everyone would know. I was a fugitive and hiding out as well. He said, "I'mma go see Dre & TB." I was puzzled. "Huh? Cuz… what? Yo, Dre robbed me and pulled on me. Yeah, let's go see him. I'mma get that chump!" Rookie said, "Nah Cuh. Those my peoples. Let me deal with it. Leave him alone. I got it." I didn't quite like what I had just heard. I was upset about it. *Did I hear him right? Did he say Dre was 'his peoples'? Did he just say to leave Dre alone and let him handle it? And on top of all that I was about to see this ni**a, even though I had plans to see this ni**a? Had the streets made me soulless?* "Cuz, I'll give you a few dollars. That's my little homie. He works for me. I started hitting him and his bro off."

We made it up Burns Heights the next afternoon after getting a ride from one of my customers. The look on Dre's face when I walked in his door behind my cuz was priceless. "Wha wha wha what what up cuz?" Was his greeting to Rook. I didn't say a word. I just stood there with my hand clutched around my pistol inside my pocket. Once again, Rook calmed everyone down. This guy was like the peacemaker unless it was him being challenged, threatened, or whatever. He, however, was a very nice person, didn't cause trouble or bother anyone unless it was joking, making jokes, being silly. Nevertheless, once he got aggravated it was on.

Times Up

The rain was beating down on the brim of my Pirate hat as we stood to wait for the police to finish his usual routine of driving through the Jet's. Something seemed a little strange though because he turned his lights out and just sat there. Then another car rolled up slowly and parked near the entrance. *What was going on?* I dipped back and pulled my pistol out and tossed it into the bushes. "Dog, you see where that is if I don't make it I'mma need you to get it and hold onto it for me." R-Dog agreed, "Alright bro." Without further thought, I slid my tall, lanky frame into the back door of B3 building. I took a quick piss and slowly walked to the third floor, tiptoeing on each step with caution, once to the top I sat gazing out the window from the corner. *Was it R-Dog who whistled to signal that the cops were headed my way? Did he try to alert me but unintentionally alert them that they were on the right track and getting closer to me.* Bubble guts kicked in on me and I had an instant urge to use the toilet, but for some eerie feeling that came over me, I knew I wouldn't be using one anytime soon unless it was in the pants I had on. As I heard the police radios, keys, and footsteps getting closer. I had the highest hopes of maybe they'll skip this entrance or wouldn't come up the stairs all the way. "He's in this hallway. Right there!" Mrs. Vale yelled from her window screaming through the fan that was in it. *What a freakin' moron!* I remained quiet though. I tried to open all the back-door apartments as they were closing in on me. Just what I assumed would happen happened. The officer rushed upstairs with his gun drawn. "Get on the floor now! Get down! Hands out where I can see them!" "I didn't do anything. Search me. I don't have anything," I said with a crackly voice. "We have a warrant for your arrest as well as a warrant from your county probation officer. You're going away for a long time, Bud." It was like a chain reaction. Rodney had just gotten picked up not long before and was sentenced to four years for shooting our star running back in the stomach. Rookie was picked up soon after and pled guilty and was sentenced to a 5 to 10-year sentence for homicide. I went back in front of Judge Williams after sitting for ten days and was sentenced to ninety days at the Academy Residential.

Ninety days at the Rez and then another six months back at the Academy!

The Rez was like a juvenile boot camp. It was located in South Park in the woods. It looked like a cabin or an old chicken farmhouse of some sort. They held approximately thirty to forty-five of the most rebellious, troubled, clueless juveniles across Allegheny County. It was staffed by college guys that surely were a part of some fraternity. The stories they told at the end of the nights or during the early morning shifts were fascinating to me.

Sean Gibson was one of the employees and what seemed like his frat brothers. They were all in good shape, full of life and certainly enjoying it. I soon found out that Mr. Gibson was the grandson of the late great baseball player, Josh Gibson, from the American Negro Baseball League. In 1972, he became the second Negro League player inducted into the National Baseball League Hall of Fame.

These frat brothers talked about the parties and the latest girl's phone numbers they got and everything else. They sat at the desks that aligned each exit door and the other doorways. Some of them could be real jerks to the kids that had an attitude or were caught sleeping during quiet time. If you were caught not doing any schoolwork, you'd stand in a corner against a brick wall or even be instructed to clean the bathroom floor with a toothbrush. I knew when to cut up and when to chill out.

Naturally, I always recognized when game was being given and learned to pay attention to detail. But there was a select few that always wanted to clown around, bug out, get restrained and sent back off to Shuman Center. Not me! I was patient and smart enough to follow the rules, remain humble, to play my part to not lose the initiation, and take charge before others do, allowing the opponent to dictate the subject.

I planned to do my ninety days here, go on the run again, and stay out until I turned eighteen, so I could let the juvenile charges get thrown out. Obviously from my plan, I didn't learn one thing except for a little math and a strategy to outlast the police for almost three years. I also planned to get back with my homie Slicc and get what was owed to me from the couple dollars I put up to get our portion rolling off the top. First, I'd have to get in shape doing calisthenics with these other juveniles being instructed by these frat brothers.

We would have our groups and one-on-one counseling sessions that were somewhat successful. I seemed to always retain a new piece of the game from a session that I would implement sometime soon. Other times, I would read the Bible that my mother sent me and mark a little notch into my wooden desk I was assigned. It was my reminder that I'm a day closer to being released.

A lot of these other juveniles in here had loud barks, but their bite wasn't vicious. They'd get smart with the counselors and stuff or other inmates but when they got called out to fight, they couldn't fight or didn't want to fight, however, the staff would restrain you quick.

When the end of the three months finally came, I was ecstatic, nervous, and ready to take on the world. I felt like it was me against the world. Everything was going according to the plan.

My homies were up though, which made my return even smoother. They didn't fumble the ball while I was gone. On my second day out, Nate T came rolling up in his T-Top Trans Am and said, "Young buck. What up? You heard what just happened?" I slowly shook my head, indicating that I didn't know what happened. He went on to say that he was sitting in the back of the Heights when Trot rolled up, put his hoodie on and ran up in TB's apartment with a tech nine trying to rob him. They were tussling over the gun while Dre was upstairs playing the video game. He heard the noise and came down with the 38 snub nose and shot Trot on his side. Trot had a bulletproof vest on, but the bullets he had went through the vest, pierced his chest and killed him.

Wow. Had I heard him clearly? Dre just killed TROT with the pistol he stole, robbed, whatever, off of me? What kind of message was this? A message from God? From the Reaper? I was shocked.

Both TB and his little brother, Dre, were arrested and charged with homicide. It wasn't long before they took the plea. Dre got juvenile life, which was about four years. TB didn't get that much time because he pled self-defense. It came out that to get the plea deal, Dre had to tell the homicide unit and the local police where he acquired the gun and everything else leading up to that day.

Was homicide coming for me, or were the local police going to harass me because he just told them I carry guns?

Chapter Eight

Now I Feel Ya

D*own. Set. Hut one. Hut two.* Sweet Pea dropped back, football tucked in his left hand, scrambling backward almost slipping in the snow that was now packed in being the turkey bowl was well into the 4th quarter. He was being pursued by Pin Head, the big burly lineman. He moved like a Michael Vick in his prime. He turned and launched a rocket, only to have it hit the tombstone of the deceased at the cemetery where we played every Thanksgiving morning. Most were snowed in, but we loved the days when we awoke to see the snowflakes and covered grounds. Everyone wanted to be the quarterback. I was just fine either watching from the side or playing free safety. Once I hit puberty, my football days were over. This particular day was memorable because not only did the whole neighborhood get together in the early morning hours, but I'd sneak in for a real meal with my mother and sister. However, the day before I got into a small disagreement with my older friend that lived in a building that sat on the corner of 2nd and Priscilla.

This particular building had two normal residents, her and my cousin Reuben's first love, Michelle. The rest were crack addicts, heroin addicts, and hustlers that loafed in the building. As it started to get late, I slowly made my way closer to the "Carter" as they called it. I wasn't going inside until everything I had on me was gone, so I sat inside the building smoking my joint. I had a key to get in her house so there wasn't any rush to get inside before she went to bed or wasn't home. Besides, I was holding my packages there. Finally, it was 2:45 am as I glanced at my pager and my customer wanted seventy worth, but I only had forty left on me. I told them to hold on and wait a minute. Skipping two to three steps at a time, I was in front of the second-floor apartment door within a second. I knocked first and didn't get an answer, so I reached deep inside my baggy Karl Kani jeans fumbling around all the dead presidents that were balled and stuffed in both front pockets, finally pulling out the key and letting myself in. Once inside, I noticed that the TV was still on. The Three Stooges were on the screen. I glanced briefly laughing before opening the bedroom door to grab my stash real quick. To my surprise, I noticed a very tall frame and some big feet hanging off the bed with my friend laying next to him. He was laying naked as if she put him to sleep with her special night-night cream. He was just snoring away. I pulled my pistol out once I noticed who it was. *Were they in a drunk sleep?* Although I wasn't making much noise, I felt as though I would have woken up if it was me.

The man who didn't budge was our local basketball and football star. I wasn't going to kill him. I'd just scare the mess out of both of them. So after getting my stash, tiptoeing over his school-issued sneakers and sweatsuit as well as boxers, socks, and t-shirts, I went back into the hallway to take care of my customer (Snap) as we called them. I returned and looked again at them lying in bed, just staring as if I was Jason or Freddie Kreuger ready to inflict torture and pain. I decided to tap my friend with the nose of my pistol first and she woke up looking like she just saw a ghost or was in the worst nightmare ever. I signaled with my finger for her to be quiet and come here. She followed my order and did just that. After getting her in the kitchen, she begged and pleaded for me not to shoot him or hurt him. I didn't have any intent on doing so anyhow, but I was going to get a good laugh in. I wasn't jealous that he was there. I was in love with money, not her.

I was becoming intoxicated with the power it was bringing. I went back in and this guy was still snoring. I grabbed his pants and underwear and then screamed, "Crump!" while tapping his long feet with the nose of my gun. After a few taps, he jumped up realizing it was me. He said, "Oh snap!" and grabbed his shoes and whatever else was left that I didn't have in my hand and ran straight out the door butt naked. I looked out the window and watched as he was standing on the sidewalk trying to get dressed. "Here fool!" I threw the rest of his clothes out of the window. From that day forward, he seemed to keep his distance from me and look the other way.

I turned my attention back to her and said, "Now I feel ya." I felt her on the previous conversations we had when she said she was tired of me messing with all the other girls and just coming to her house late night and not wanting to do anything except have sex. She said she was tired and was going to get back with her old boyfriend. I turned my key in that day and never looked back. I moved on without a second thought. I was back at it, night after night, pulling all-night shifts. I started having the urge to drive, so I bought another vehicle, which I only had for three weeks before it was impounded. Rent-a-Rock became my daily routine. Renting a car for a rock. These were the days when drug addicts were high functioning; enjoy getting high, drive nice vehicles, work and a family. Sort of like how the tech giants in Silicon Valley are now. The difference was in Duquesne, it was the steel mill rather than the ocean and border.

Times Up

Here I was approaching my sixteenth birthday in less than thirty days and my time on the run had come to an end. Not sure what it was with these old folks in the projects where I grew up, but once again, someone had called the police on me. This time it was Mr. Woody. He talked to me as if nothing was happening, but just as the police pulled into the projects, he grabbed me and held me as they approached the scene. Maybe because he despised me for always selling to his older son, or the late nights near his window making noise all night long. Whatever the case was, I ended up back at Shuman Center. It was evident that I violated my probation and court order, went AWOL again, and so I was soon headed for a long vacation. I would've never in a million years thought that it would be my last time seeing those two buildings standing; the very last time I'd step foot in those urine smelling hallways; last time I'd see Erie Pirl's apartment. No more sitting around hustling with the fellas, drinking 40 ounces of Old English, Red and Blue Bull. No more chilling with the old heads Clarkie G, Terry Flash, Ms. Lokey's with Big Meech, Speedy John, and Little ID. No more sneaking up to old head Clemies when her kids were sleeping. No more shooting craps into the wee hours of the morning. Just that fast it was being taken away from me. My freedom, my family, and my friends. My faith was the only thing I had.

After a rigorous time, I had a hearing and was sentenced to one year at the George Junior Republic, a facility about an hour and a half away from home. It's one of the nation's largest private non-profit residential treatment facilities. GJR houses, schools, and disciplines five hundred high school boys from troubled backgrounds. They use a behavior and education treatment model and provide psychological testing, evaluations, vocational training, recreation, and athletics. They have cottages that house the boys. The homes were modern and gave the campus the appearance of an upper-class housing development.

So, to say the least, I finally got my education and diploma within that time frame. It was there where I learned to accept no for an answer. They had a point system that determined every move you made. I humbled myself, focused, and made the best of the situation. Once I earned my first visit, I was really alright. My mom brought my female friend up with her to visit me, and boy oh boy it was a nice visit. We even got to leave campus for a little bit. I thanked my mom profusely for that visit and the others. I was able to get loose… all the way loose if you know what I mean.

While at GJR, I found out that I liked horses. Yes, they had horses, and I took to them and the super-hot lady that wore skintight jeans that hugged her frame just as good as the yoga pants do nowadays with the women.

I seemed to adapt quickly to my new home. Time went pretty fast. Slicc caught a big drug case and ended up going to Vision Quest, which was much stricter than GJR. I passed a lot of my time reading books and magazines. Some were science, algebra, and social studies books. Culinary arts interested me somewhat. Carpentry seemed to keep my attention much more, though.

There were boys from Philly that were pretty darn good that were on the basketball team. The hoop team went undefeated. Wayne Butler was one of the young men that were on the team. He ended up coming to Pittsburgh from Philly and never left. He made it his hometown. Larry Luv was another. He was from my neighborhood, and we were about the same age.

Larry was already at GJR when I got there, so he showed me some things when I first showed up on campus. All in all, the experience was helpful. It taught me how to remain patient; it instilled discipline within me; and more importantly, I learned to accept NO for an answer. I became accountable for my actions, took full responsibility and figured out that there was much more to life that I had to prepare for.

I studied the Bible faithfully. I learned so much about the beginning of time and the sacrifices that Jesus made for us. I even realized and learned that God would forgive me for the foolish things that I had done over the last few years since my pre-teen days.

After all the Sunday schools and Bible studies I participated in while going with Reuben and his stepfather, Brother Daryl, I didn't grasp the knowledge and understanding the way I started to when I'd study and read by myself during quiet time or before bed when I felt lonely, confused, misunderstood, and vulnerable. I found comfort, self-worth, peace, and a sense of direction when I was tuned in to God. However, the difficult part I found was the temptation that lurked around and near me daily. Whether I was sitting at my desk in our multi-bedrooms, being tempted by the roommate who was smoking marijuana and cigarettes or passing a dirty magazine my way to just simply breaking the rules. Temptation at a small level to lusting off the staff, to what the outside world would be on another level.

Chapter Nine

Better Learn About the Dress Code

Here I was on my way back to the Greyhound station after a weekend visiting pass home. I waited until the very last hour for Nate T to drive me back. We hadn't made it past Kennywood yet on the boulevard and he was speeding trying to race against time. He hit a corner and t-boned out; we spun completely around almost hitting head-on with a Port Authority bus that was heading in the opposite direction coming towards us. The only thing that saved us was the Lord once again. He spun the vehicle back around and continued despite the clicking noise that had become loud, probably from hitting the curb as we first approached the turn. He found a way to get me there on time though, just a few minutes before departure. That was a long quiet ride back to GJR. I did a lot of soul-searching and thinking about my weekend. *I can't wait 'til these last thirty days are up.*

On the visit home, I noticed Nate T, who was ET and Rooskie's older brother, had started lounging with Slicc and our crew. He was Slicc's brother's age, like eight years older than us. He said we were his young boys from the Jet's. We even put in a little work over in Clairton while I was on my weekend visit.

So yeah, I allowed the devil to take back over that fast. Seemed as though I hadn't learned anything. I had just done almost a year and went right back to the same thing. *Did I need to face the fact that I was just a product of my environment? Would I ever really change? Had I just made excuses to go back? Had I been blind to reality? Had demons taken over my spirit? Or had I just simply not matured? Maybe I needed more time to reflect and learn. Maybe the sentence wasn't stern enough. Or maybe I needed a change of environment.*

Well, I soon got a change of environment after I got released. I came home and got into a shootout in broad daylight. I robbed Mareese in front of the gambling joint and was getting many others who wrongly crossed into my path. My mother said she couldn't handle me and that I was going to end up dead or in jail for a long time if I didn't settle down. I didn't believe that at all. I knew it all, and nobody could tell me anything. I took care of myself; even if it was at somebody else's expense.

After pleas to do something with me from my mother, saying I was thugged out, my brother ended up coming back home for what seemed like to save me and get me out of the way. It just so happened that he got an honorable discharge for whatever reason. Maybe it was all just God's work.

It was true. I had become a thug. I even had that phrase tattooed on my forearm, "ALL THUG." I idolized Tupac, and everything I heard him say I picked up on it and was trying to live it. I seemed to relate to every single verse. Maybe I listened to him as I would've my father had he been around.

My brother came back and brought along this lady with him from Germany where he was based. Then he left her and found a new lady in East Liberty off of Larimer Ave. She had two sons and a daughter. The oldest son was Berto. He was about two years older than me. Then there was Colt, who was my age. The daughter was a little younger by just a year. Trying to get me on track and into a different environment seemed logical and worth a try. But what they didn't realize was that these boys on Larimer Ave. were way more advanced and thuggin' just as much. My brother had to know that and did know that!

I soon found out that he was selling himself. He put down the combat boots and slipped into a pair of Timberlands. Instead of going to get his license to carry, he decided to carry without a license. I came down and blended right in. I was welcomed with open arms and soon hit the Ave, which was just in an eyes sight, maybe a forty-five-second walk from the house on Meadow. I thank Berto and Colt for teaching me the way they did things. It was very different. No more rocks being placed inside of Tylenol or medicine bottles; it was strictly double pleated baggies. The rocks were wrapped in those and placed in your mouth about five at a time. Spitting dubs all day and night became the new thing. Carrying guns wasn't new to me and we didn't carry them all the time when I first moved down there. Not until late at night, or when our old head B would load us up in his conversion van and take us from city to city jumping out on the new Bloods and Crips gang members while they were on the corners shooting dice, drinking, hustling, or whatever.

I'll tell you what, the element of surprise is something else. We all would jump out at the same time, pistols drawn, and it was every man (or kid) for himself. Grab what you can and it's yours. We would dress in all black, nothing else. You had to participate, or you would get dealt with the next day. Big B always knew who wasn't rolling, also.

We had all acquired mountain bikes to get around faster and be more elusive from the guys trying to retaliate and doing drive-by shooting at us and the task force riding in Chevy Celebrities and Impalas. I can remember the first time I was harassed by them. I had just stepped off the porch, literally. Fresh out of the shower wearing my favorite jean outfit, a Damage jean jacket, and pants. I'd wear that every other day that I wasn't wearing my all black t-shirt and khaki Dickie pants with my all black ACG's or Timberlands. As soon as I hit the bottom step leading to the cracked-up sidewalk that looked like it hadn't been cared for since the '70s maybe, I made eye contact with Poncho the light-skinned undercover cop that was in the passenger seat. He immediately signaled his partner, Conan, to stop the vehicle. Just as he did, I tried to turn to go back up the steps to the house and he yelled, "Freeze!" My scream was loud and full of panic "For what??? I didn't do anything." In the same moment, in the same breath, I swallowed five double-ups of pure yellow crack. Poncho was on my back in a quick flash with his knee in my back saying, "Don't move!"

Here I was on the porch of my new residence, still being harassed by the law who were supposed to be protecting the citizens, not stereotyping a teenager in front of their home. Within a short time, Ms. Chelle opened the door and all I could hear her yell was, "Get off him! What in the world are you doing? He isn't bothering anyone. I sent him to the store for milk and cereal. What the hell are you doing?" "I know exactly who he is and what he's doing!" Poncho exclaimed in return. "We saw him in these same clothes two days ago selling to some crack addict. He saw us and fled between Paulson and the Ave. We've been watching your home." "You can watch all you want, but right now he's going to the store and you're on my property assaulting a teenage child. What's your badge number?" he continued searching my pants pockets and in between my crotch. Little did he realize and know it was already sliding down my esophagus and into my stomach.

Ms. Chelle knew exactly what time it was. She just told me to be careful as I was getting ready to go out. Just as she and my brother must've had a date night planned because she was all in the mirror looking like a straight up and down TEN! Yes, she was gorgeous and had the perfect personality to match. I honestly thought way back then that she was the one my brother would marry and grow old with. I would soon learn very different, as their relationship dwindled right before my eyes. He would go days without coming home and when he was around it was just long enough to shower, and he'd be right back out after asking was I alright. It eventually came to the point where he was never there, and I was just alright with that because I was enjoying my new family. They welcomed me with open arms and continued to, even though my bro had done their mother not so well towards the end. Berto and Colt ("Four Pound") never switched up. They always kept it real as real can get. They were my brothers from another mother, and I found that out on several occasions when it got so real. I can't begin to go into any details. Just know that when it was time, I knew I could look their way and on one particular evening I did in a major way.

We gooned up one day to load up and head to the Duke after I got into it with the Dirty Pimp about a situation with Slicc. A forty-five-minute ride for us from East Liberty must've only taken twenty minutes because my bros were pulling up ten cars deep in a matter of time. It was a huge crowd that had gathered around. Nobody was prepared to see fifteen pistols, fifteen hoodlums in all black ready to put in some work. I was told to point him out, after walking through the crowd and not seeing the DP, I gave the "it's cool. He's not here now" signal. But before we got back into the cars to head out, one of the homies screamed out, "If we gotta come back out here, we gone light the whole block up!" A series of "Gow! Gow! Gow!" filled the air as that was our call. We jumped in the whips and rolled out. From that very day moving forward, my reputation changed again in the Duke. Now all the old drug dealers that were standing out in the projects when we came through that day respected me, and the word was, "Clabo ain't no joke. That little young boy freaking crazy. Young boy 'bout it!"

I sensed a changed from pretty much the whole city. *Was I ego trippin'? Maybe... maybe not.* Maybe I was to an extent. However, the bottom line was, I was worse than ever now, especially being I found my way back over there more and more now. It wasn't just about me running around being a little hoodlum. I was being introduced to a new thing that put me so far out of touch with reality, but in my mind as a seventeen year old hanging around with the older homies, drinking 40s, shooting dice, and gaining attention from more girls than ever, this seemed to be the best life ever.

My days soon became getting up at the sound of a beeping horn. I'd grab my pager and see that 007 with a 30 behind it, or a message or word that only could be read by turning the pager the opposite way. Or a 357 which meant Paula want the big 50 bags "brick" for a whopping 30 dollars per bag. Waking up to a $1,500 page was lovely, I thought. This is the life. While most of the homies I grew up with were headed to school I was walking the total opposite way headed to Ash Alley or the alley behind my mother's apartment or even right on Crawford Ave. It didn't matter. I would get it any way I could, wherever I could.

Most days before noon, I was sold out of everything fronted to me. Yes, I was working off of front's now. Simply because the old heads kept their game tight, wasn't messy, kept their connect private, and had everyone go through them at this point. I didn't think to ask could I get a cheaper price or send my couple thousand I saved despite my gambling addiction and everything else I was indulging in. I was able to get it a little cheaper from ET. Yes, the guy who I saw riding past me on my way to school years ago in that brand new 5.0 green Mustang convertible was now my new connect. He'd give me five packs for $4,500. I'd turn those over in a day and a half, two days was on slow days or days I had to grind it all out because I was gambling with them and lost. Man! Those were sometimes right there! I'd lose then go hustle all night long, selling the dubs that sold all night in projects due to the epidemic that took place in almost every black community in the United States. *Were these states really united?* Certainly didn't seem so in my eyes. I wasn't blind to that!

By noon, my day was slowing down. I'd go shower or to be honest, maybe it was a birdbath. You know at the sink hurrying to wash the most sacred places on your body. All the special cracks and crevices on your body; under your arms, below your waist, and between the toes, then back out the door I'd go, off to Burns Heights. I'd be posted back up with my pistol, and a fresh blunt rolled up.

Sports became non-existent unless I was rolling with the old heads to a high school hoop game or something. One particular evening while in attendance at one of the local hoop games in the nearby town of Homestead, PA, God was trying to slow me down, but of course, I didn't listen.

Before we headed out for the big hoop game, the day consisted of sitting under the yum yum tree, drinking Thunderbird with Kool-Aid, Red Bull and Blue Bull 40 ounces, and even Old English 800 was being passed around freely. For some strange reason, I decided to drink a little of it all and clung to a bottle of Mad Dog 20/20. In comparison, that tasted like a cold glass of sweet tea from McDonald's or Hawaiian Punch. By the time we got into the cars to head over, I must've passed out in the back seat of Pete's Eagle. They somehow managed to wake me up upon arriving at the school. I walked into that gym head spinning and staggering all between the bleachers before finally taking a tumble. The next time I remember anything was the moment I woke up with a bright light in my face strapped to a hard metal frame, tubes in my mouth and nose, and my mother standing alongside me with tears in her eyes mumbling a conversation with God. I tried pulling the tube out my throat only to realize my arms were not budging. I was confined (restrained) to the metal frame. All I knew was that my throat was burning, and my stomach was in so much pain with an aching sensation. "Boy do you realize what just happened?" my mother asked softly. "No, ma'am." "You just had your stomach pumped."

Soon after, a doctor came in and explained that I was rushed into the ER for severe intoxication and was near death from alcohol poisoning. I had to be rushed into an emergency procedure to have my stomach pumped. Where were my so-called homies or friends right now? Well to be perfectly honest, some were probably still on the basketball court playing in the game. Maybe I should've, could've, would've stuck to sports, but I didn't. I tried my hand at another game, and it wasn't baseball, basketball, nor football. This was a dangerous game. A game that'll take your life in the blink of an eye. A game where no slipping was allowed. A game that only the strong survived. A game that the ball bounced all over the place and there was hardly ever an out of bounds. A game where there were no rules and if there were, they were never followed. The only game I knew that you can have however many people you wanted to have on your team. A game that would put you so far deep inside the game that you could become blind to basic things. The game would have you out of touch with reality. The game that where you ran more than a hundred yards for a touchdown, the endzone may never be in sight.

As I was led out of the hospital hours later, it felt as if the whole earth was spinning as I stepped slowly towards the Ford LTD passenger side door. The whole walk to the car and most memorably the ride home, my mother laid into me verbally. But all I could think of was a bed, a couch, the home I was so grateful to see. She expressed her sorrows for her wrongdoings and reminded me of the embarrassment I inflicted on the entire family. She said she was scared for me because I was out of control and needed to get a grip on life. She'd scream on me then just stared and whisper, "Boy, God had you covered since you were in my womb." Would she repeat that phrase anymore? Would I shape up, see the light, and get things right? Or would I continue on the path I was on?

The Takeover

It wouldn't take long to see that nothing had changed because two days later we were several carloads deep riding on River Road Route 837 on our way over to C-Town, Clairton PA, for our season finale. This had to be one of the most competitive, hyped up rivalries in Western PA at the time in the early 1990s. The huge speakers and amplifier that was in the trunk of the car had my ears ringing. "Cream Get the Money Dolla Dolla Bill Y'all" Wu-Tang Clan was being mixed in with some KRS-One at the same time. Def Sef had just cut Volume #6 Mixtape. I tapped Nate T on the shoulder and said, "Man, put that Jay-Z on," and immediately "It's a Hard Knock Life" came whistling through the kicker speaker system. We pulled up at the game room, I didn't see a school anywhere. I was looking around like, I thought we were going to the game. Oh, we were. We just made a stop beforehand to do a walk through and see the young ladies that may have been standing around looking for some attention from a young handsome guy like myself or one of my old heads that were wearing fat gold chains, with Duke Blue Devil sweatshirts. Me, Butters, Slicc, R-Dog, Speedy John Pirl, Nate T, and Pete Hawk were walking through the game room as a few guys from Clairton shot pool and started whispering amongst themselves. I observed the whole situation. I had every one of them counted for with the 9mm I had on my hip, enough to let every single one of them borrow a bullet. That was my way of thinking. Although we were just coming to watch a game and enjoy ourselves, my mentality was something different. Maybe because everything I had done so far in my short life. Or was I a soft kid who was afraid to throw his hands up? Not at all, I had gotten into plenty of fights growing up. In the meantime, I kept a close eye on this guy that was a little stocky and looked like he had an attitude. He was mean mugging and grittin' in our direction. So I told Nate T, "Check this fool out. I'll light him up. Somebody better check him." Slicc said, "Chill Clabo. My cuz said he's always tryna start some mess with somebody." Slicc was in a conversation with a kid that looked to be a hustler or something because it wasn't but a minute after that a crackhead ran up to him and said, "Rex, I have eighty bucks, please hook me up." Then a second later a dark-skinned, thick thighed, big booty girl came walking up to us and said, "What up cuz?" Rex nodded in reply, "What up cuz?" As Rex turned to head out, Slicc followed, we all formed a line and rolled behind him. I was last and kept my eye on the kid with the attitude, making sure I didn't lose eye contact with him. As I would've bet that wouldn't be the last time we'd see each other…

Upon getting outside and walking to the side parking lot, we nearly surround this all-black Grand National with Dayton rims on it. Oh my! This car was glistening in the night lights. Rex, I noticed was a cool kid and not because of the car, but because he shook and gave that brotherly love hug to every one of us and said he'd see us at the game. On the ride to the school, Speedy John says to me, "Bro, that dark skin chick wants you. Her girl told me. Her name is Wendy." "Oh yeah?" I replied. "I'll knock her down. She's super thick."

We got to the game and sure enough, as I had said to myself, Rex was a cool kid. He came and sat by us as he later mentioned that he didn't mess with too many boys over that way and on occasions, we'd find out who was who and what was what because from that day forward we were hanging at the game room and the projects or wherever the girls invited us to. Clairton soon became our second home. We all met girls over there and started meeting more people. Some good folks, some haters, some hustlers, some mothers. I met the whole family; mom, dad, brothers, cousins, aunts, uncles, everyone because I started staying overnight with Wendy.

I always laugh and tell them I started making them carry guns in Clairton, which was true. I started robbing anyone who my boy put me onto. Anyone he didn't like or said, "Get him," I would lurk where I was told to, that being their apartment or mother's home or simply in broad daylight or after hours or on consignment, whatever, or, however. I was on it. Then I started putting my homies on the same thing. Before long, we had beef with a few of them. One is the guy from the game room that had the attitude. The thing about him that I found out was he was the neighborhood bully and many young men didn't even like him.

A couple of months went past; a few house parties, block parties, and state championship titles later, my class of '94 went on to become the undefeated Class A champions in football and state champs in basketball. I'm not sure if that would've happened if I didn't give our star standout quarterback and 6'6 dominant basketball player Crump a free pass that night when I caught him in the bed with my friend and woke him up out of his sleep. That goes to show that once again I had the devil on one shoulder shouting bad thoughts, evil intentions lurking and on the right shoulder, God was still holding me tightly staying with me every step of the way.

We were back and forth from the Duke to Clairton every day almost. I stopped hanging in the City with my Larimer Ave boys, but would occasionally stop through to conduct some business on multiple levels. I kept in touch with a few of the homies for quite some time until they were hit with the RICO ACT after joining forces with another neighborhood instead of staying to themselves. They did something really stupid to attract the FBI, they call themselves LAW!!! which stood for Larimer and Wilkinsburg. That was the wrong move I still believe to this day.

Wendy and I remained very good friends. Eventually, I started messing with a couple of different women that were older than me by several years and a couple about my age. I sort of started becoming a little player. What Ludacris say? He had girls in different area codes. Well in Pittsburgh, it was all 412-area code, so I'll say I had 'em in every zip code. Not proud or bragging about it but you have to understand I was a handsome son of a gun. Most times women would approach me, flirt with me, or whatever. I struggled with that. My problem was I very rarely didn't act on the persuasion. One of our favorite sayings amongst the fellas was, "I caught her peeking at me." With Wendy and I still being friends, I started seeing this Puerto Rican girl named Lasette. Not quite sure how that even evolved but nine times out of ten, I'll bet that she got caught peeking. Whether it was the bar I was too young to be in or the local corner store. She had an apartment in the projects along with a little 6-month-old baby. That became our trap house, party house, and everything else. We'd shoot something up, rob something or somebody, and then make our way to her apartment… our safe haven in Clairton!

Nate T, our old head, had an apartment, well a girl with an apartment not too far from me. But his girl didn't play all that craziness. She was in college studying law. Maybe she saw the potential with all the foolishness we were into. We started going to this night club called the Hollywood Club in Clairton. Age didn't matter. You could get in as long as you knew the right person. We always found a way to slide in.

The Hollywood Club attracted people from every surrounding city, which became a big problem eventually. The reason being was guys from McKeesport hung out there also, to be quite specific, AK the guy who we put that heat on, robbed and took his puppy years ago. He blew up in the game and had a gang of guys he hung out with.

One evening we all were in the club together and we locked eyes. It was on from there. I had a new .38 snub-nose revolver in my Timberland boot, though. Well, it started in my boot. Once inside, I'd go to the bathroom and put it in my pocket. I never wanted to get caught slippin'. The way things were going now it was highly likely being we were in the club with all our enemies, it was about to go down. We were playing a dangerous game. To make matters worse, Clairton and McKeesport got along well. It was just this little group of hoodlums, my squad, that was always into something no good and they didn't like it. The women seemed to like it though because we had a couple of them each.

One night we left the club and gunshots rang out all over the parking lot. There were holes in numerous vehicles and the news was called. Not sure what it was about that club, but the very next weekend everyone gathered at the spot again. We drank at Lasette's and played some spades. I told the boys I was chillin' and they all should chill out also; don't go to the club; it's hot and somebody is going to get killed. So, I stayed in, I might've been a bit crazy, but I wasn't stupid. I knew how to do my dirt and get away with it. I was never the one to run into a traffic jam knowing its rush hour. I'll take the side streets or wait 'til traffic die down. It simply didn't make common sense to me to go back the very next weekend after a major shootout the week before!

I wasn't able to talk them out of it, so they went on and I chilled out with Lasette. We cleaned up the apartment and went to bed. At 1:53 am the house phone rang. Just the ring alone didn't sound right as it startled me out of my sleep. Have you ever heard your phone ring and before you knew who was on the other line, you knew who it was or knew and felt that something wasn't right? Nowadays everyone has the option with smartphones to enable different ring tones for every person in their contact list. But back then, that wasn't an option. I picked the phone up with a sleepy, "Hello." On the other line Butter's was screaming, "Get his gun out his pocket! Back up, let him breathe!"

"Clabo. Clabo! Dog, Pirl got shot, he's shot in the stomach." I asked where they were and who did it. His reply was, "Clabo, just please come get us. We're on our way up the hill walking. We're dirty and Pirl is getting life flighted downtown." I grabbed the keys and darted out the door, jumped in the whip and sped out. I rode near the club and lights lit up the street. Yellow tape nearly blocked off the whole parking lot. My homies were nowhere in sight. So, I continued driving around. To my surprise, I couldn't find anyone, so I went back to Lasette's only to open the door and have all the fella's sitting around talking. After a few minutes, it became clear what had happened. As they were leaving the club in the parking lot, the Mckeesport boys ambushed the homies and Pirl was caught in the crossfire. Pirl didn't carry a gun, and he wasn't a bad person. He missed his calling because he should've been a comedian. Everyone laughed with him anytime he was around. He just was hanging with the wrong group of friends. I'm not saying he didn't do anything wrong but overall, he was a good kid.

I went and visited him in the days after. God kept him close. He pulled through. He just would have to wear a colostomy bag for a couple of months but should make a full recovery per the doctor's words. Things heated up for a while afterward. I'll leave it like that.

We stayed around continued hanging out. Just a mere few days later something really sad happened after drinking at Lasette's apartment with her girlfriends and my homies. We all stayed over that night and in the wee hours of the morning she jumped out of the bed from our sleep and screamed and ran to the baby screaming at the top of her lungs "My baby! My baby!" A mother's intuition is really deep. She picked up her baby out of the bassinet as I stood behind her. The baby was stiff and colorless. She turned and ran down the steps and straight out the door. I tried running behind her, but she kept running. The baby had passed away from SIDS. That was a very sad time. It freaked me out. She wasn't the same anymore after that, which I understood. I stayed around as long as I could and as long as she allowed and wanted me to. But I respected her home and space and fell back a bit, eventually, we parted ways over time.

I begin to wonder why trouble lurked everywhere I was. I begin to speak with God out loud at times. Just asking God to please help me, guide me, save me. But still, I was allowing the blind to lead the blind. I felt like I had the weight of the world on my shoulder.

Bars became the everyday thing for me, some days for opening and every day in the evenings. With a bar on every corner in the whole city, the city was lit, and everything was a go. The problem with that was I was underage frequenting these establishments at just a young seventeen years. Once some of those local tavern owners realized I wasn't a problem due to the money we were spending, we agreed that I'd stay only in the restaurant/cooking area just in case the LCB or local police decided to come through the bar. For some strange reason, they always seemed to come into the minority-owned establishments when I was inside. But when I'd go to the other Caucasian owned taverns, I could stay all night, hustle, drink, and keep it open later than normal business hours. I did get myself barred from the Elks.

Ruthless & Reckless

I implemented that we all start wearing black every day on the block; a tradition I carried on since leaving Larimer Ave. Then we decided to use the name that held all these establishments and homes and claim the street as our street or block with a renaming ceremony and joining of homies officially calling ourselves the PA Gangstas. I lived on the Ave. Pulling all-nighters and gambling playing C-Lo hitting licks all night long. We all came together, or so I thought, I'll take the credit for joining my everyday homies that were strictly thuggin' with my other old head homies. They were getting' money. The same ones that were riding in brand new Mustangs and Mercedes Benz years before, it was me, Bowie City, Pirl, Slicc, R-Dog, Butters, G-Fight, PinHead, The Dirty Pimp, Tone B, CY, Rooskie,Ric Scott, Sweet Pea, Chilly Fat, ET, Flash, Nate-T, and Doc Boog. Then we had another few young boys. Tobey and big Tay and em. There are some old heads that I didn't mention. Most of these guys played baseball together, grew up down the Jets and slept over one another's home at some point. I brought us together and kicked a couple off the squad somewhat. A little distance grew amongst a couple after I pulled out my pistol in the bathroom of the Elks bar and let off one shot striking Butters in the butt. Why did I do that? What had I done? My homie? Why would I do such a thing? Was I insane? Had someone spiked my drink? Yes, he was my homie. Yes, I was under the influence of liquor. But why did I do it? Because I was so out of control, hot-headed, and searching for a one-way ticket to prison or down below the ground.

Thanks to the Good Lord, Butters didn't die, and he didn't press any charges on me. He didn't try to retaliate either. He left God's work in God's hands. With my birthday soon approaching, he spared me seeing my eighteenth birthday. Had that bullet hit a main artery or been up in the extremities, I could've been doing a life sentence and not being able to be a father to my first-born son, Jaquan, that Wendy was soon expecting. Yep, she was very fertile, young, and tender just as I was at seventeen years old when we decided to act and participate in things as if we were established adults.

In the days to come, I continued the daily routine I was on the block so much that my puppy, Faces, would break out of the fence at my mom's home and come up to the Avenue, which was about a 25-minute walk from my mother's house. I'd get a call, or someone would come in Swamps and say, "Clabo, Faces is outside sitting on the steps." This American Terrier was smart. The heck with all the negative feedback about pit bulls. This bull was kind, gentle, and loving and had more smarts than some German Shepherds.

The same ways my puppy dog followed my every move, is the same way the younger kids were watching my every move whether I realized it or not. Was this just a vicious cycle that trickled down from one generation to the next? It sure seemed that way.

With all the robbing and hustling night and day, I was able to acquire my first motorcycle along with another car. *The game was on now*, I thought. I became so immune to the lifestyle and infatuated with the power and attention it brought, I'd do just about anything to maintain it. Maintaining was all that I was doing. Equivalent to today's working and living check to check for the average household, my 401K was the gambling joint and my hustler's mentality at the time was spend every bit of the profit. As long as I had my flip money, I was alright with that. Was I progressing or regressing? Was I in the way? After I lost a couple of grand gambling, I'd ask myself that question over and over again.

My old head homie, ET, would win most times. His luck was amazing. You'd almost think he was cheating somehow. Maybe it was just that. His money was so much longer than everyone else's he played against, he could implement a different strategy. He'd beat me and then front me the same amount that I came with to spend on that work. I was so reckless without any responsibilities quite yet and not a worry in the world.

Bowie City, another one of the old heads from our block, had a bonded relationship with this lady name Anitra. Anitra had a daughter named Tamara. She was a couple of years younger than me. Anitra was cool, she actually would be in her little world doing her thing. She loved her some Bowie City. After a few times being around with him sitting around the house, I caught Tamara peeking at me a time or two, and that was all she wrote. Bowie came downstairs one day and said, "Let's go, Clabo." When we got into his red GT, I asked him what was up with Tamara and said that she was really pretty, and I think she likes me. He said, "She's young, but go ahead and talk to her." That was all I had to hear was that approval from him, being that he was playing stepdaddy.

Later that evening, we went back, and I broke the ice with her, then immediately put her to the test by asking her to hold something for me. Since we pretty much lived around the corner from each other, I started spending plenty of time with her.

Anitra was one of the coolest mothers. She allowed me to stay nights in Tamara's room and was welcomed any day and time. I started catching serious feelings for her, even though she was just a tad bit hardheaded. She was a virgin when I met her and soon took her virginity, which seemed to drive her nuts about me. My only concern was that I knew I wasn't ready to settle down and be a one-woman man just yet. I was living my best life and how would I allow any girl, lady, woman, or anyone for that matter, to dictate or tell me what I was or was not going to do when I hardly listened to my mother?

Besides, I was using my sister's apartment she had over the barbershop to mess with other girls. I was so out of control.

I had strong feelings for this young beautiful lady. I had just came into her home and took over without her going out even looking for anything. Trouble came knocking on her door, unfortunately, her mother didn't protect her the way she should've. Broken households cause broken pieces to fall all over the place. Instability causes stress, stressed individuals do things and make rash decisions that they wouldn't do if they were in the normal state of mind. Allowing temptation to sift through and then sin kick in typically.

We as young Black adults don't give ourselves a chance to develop into what full potential will reveal. Truth be told, Tamara and I became crazy about one another to the point we tripped out on each other and others. However, I wanted my cake and others but didn't want her to have others. That's how the game went. That's what I learned from watching my old head homies at work.

In a span of two weeks, I was grazed by a bullet that ended up just millimeters from my heart because of a jealous guy that tried running up to my car because his girlfriend was on the loose. Was I treating women this way because I felt abandoned by my mother being on the go? Or was it because I didn't have a father around to teach me the proper way a man (a real man) is supposed to love his woman and respect the lady he's with or not with? Would I continue this vicious cycle that seemed to plague my home and my friend's homes and families?

Looking back, 85% of the projects consisted of broken homes, single-parent mothers of families with at least three siblings or more. Was this by design? Had the government staged the community for failure? Or was this the choice our parents made? Maybe a combination of both. I knew one thing; I had a plan and it didn't have standing still in it.

I do not know my biological father, but he must have been a go-getter because I was sure ambitious. Nobody had to push me out. I was out every chance I had. Rain, sleet, snow, and definitely sunshine. I think I stood in the rain so much that I now love the rain, sort of like my best days. I knew one thing for sure I made a commitment to myself for life that I'd break this vicious cycle in my family and make sure I'd do everything in my control to be around for my son that was just weeks away from being born.

After sitting in my mom's basement with the door to the outside cracked open for the smoke to exit without her smelling it from the huge cigar filled with green leaves, I thought to myself long and hard that I was going to man up and change some things in my life. The only problem was deciding when to change the situations that I allowed to set me back, stay stuck in the hood and become a product of the environment and become another statistic.

Chapter Ten

Lord Guide Me Save Me

Here we are riding around in the white SS hittin' licks all day. We were on our way shopping for the party I was having at a bar for my 18th birthday. Yes, a party I was throwing for myself at 18 in a local bar in the hood. Geto Boys had just dropped a new album summer of '95. It was obvious that I hadn't quite grasped that I had a newborn son that was just a couple of months old and the promise I made to myself to step up, man up and be there for Wendy and my son always. In between time, things had progressed. I was now saving more money and becoming disciplined with the reckless spending and gambling, maybe because of the responsibility of a kid and partly because my old heads I was hanging out with Flash, Doc Boog, and ET was strictly business riding in nice fancy cars, Saab's, Cadillac's, and Mercedes Benz. I had to step my game up asap. Here we are on a hot summer day, my day, my birthdate in August, I just purchased a Tim Duncan college basketball outfit top and shorts. That was in style in '95, throwbacks and jerseys. I still have a Jim Brown throwback from the Cleveland Browns, a team that living in Pittsburgh was a no-no to wear. I look back and laugh at how big we wore our clothes and the idea that I purchased that being I'm a die-hard Steelers fan.

We made a call to Clairton to see Jiggity Joe Joe to pick-up some exotic fruity stank stank. We all wanted 100 sacks that was pretty much all he sold. I made the call and Doc drove while ET was in the passenger seat. I called out the turn by turn navigation that was stored in my head. Back in '95, there wasn't any Google for this or that. You better know where you wanted to go or else you might end up on a one-way road to a dead-end or something.

After stopping past talking to Wendy, dropping a few dollars off, and talking baby talk to my first-born son, I encountered my brother-in-law JJ on the way out the door and that was right on time because he was ready to re-up on those packs. I started being able to get at my request in larger quantities being I was with the sources every day and bringing a sense of security to the table.

Once we got back to the Duke, I got dropped off at my girl's home. We sat and talked; I showered and got right then Bowie City came in making noise. "Where's Clabo? Happy Birthday, Clabo. We gettin' it in today. Let's go fire something up! I got some cold ones on ice in the cooler outback. Let's go! It's on!" The party was officially on. While sitting around talking, Tamara informed me to please not be angry, but Beez had approached her and was trying to get with her. This was some kid from NYC supposedly who found his way to the Duke after being on the run in NYC, according to the stories that floated around the hood. He hung out with my cousin Reub's squad down just adjacent from Priscilla Ave. They were jealous of all of us. It seemed they managed to get a little group of just beginning teenagers to start hating on us and brainwashing them. We should've never allowed him to relocate to the area along with Sheen.

So, after the conversation with Tamara, I became extremely pissed off. Nobody disrespected me. *Was he crazy? Was he ready for what I had in store? Did he realize she was loyal to me at that moment and time?* I told Bowie City about it and then the rest of the homies I told once they started coming around the house. We passed blunt after blunt around one after another all night. We had Hennessey by the gallon as that was the drink preferred amongst us. The latest Scarface and Tupac song blasted from the speaker that Anitra had placed in the dining room window facing the yard. After a burger and a few Heinekens along with a cup of Henny and all the smoking, I decided to ease my way out the house and jumped in my Regal with the T-Tops open and a pistol under my seat and sped off. Where was I headed? Driving under the influence! Oh, I had an agenda and it wasn't to go get ice or blunts or to sell anything. It was to find Beez and make him pay for what he had done. Disrespecting me came with a price tag or possibly a toe tag!

My intentions weren't good at all. In my mind, the second I saw him I was jumping out and doing a Beenie Sco. My first stop was on South Second Street where he was known to frequent with the other kids along with their little pit bulls. As I approached, I noticed a small group gathered near the corner of the Carter Building. I pulled up, threw the car in park, and jumped out with my pistol visibly gripped in my right hand. As I approached, Reub was already walking in my direction saying "Cuz, chill. What's up? Who you want?" I replied, "Beez. Cuz, that boy gotta go!" "Cuz, he's not even here. I haven't seen him all day. Cuz what's up? What he do? You want me to take care of it, Cuz? Let me deal with him. I'll smack his little chump behind up!"

I let him know exactly what happened and that I would catch him sooner or later, and that I had to handle that. I told my cousin Reub to come through later I was having a party at the Safari Club tonight. I made a little eye contact with his boys before jumping back in my whip, turning the Geto Boys music as loud as it could go, and flooring the pedal to the metal and flew up the hill. I proceeded on the prowl for the little weasel that disrespected me. Somehow, I ended up in Burns Heights in front of Doo Doo Bruce's house talking to them letting them know the party was on. Although they probably couldn't get in being, they were my age. Everyone couldn't do what I managed to do as far as that underage drinking in the bars. Wasn't by surprise everyone seemed to gravitate towards the taverns being as young kids walking past each corner and block that's all we saw. We'd peek inside or simply glance when a door was propped open. Maybe let out a scream or something to irritate the folks inside and then run off laughing hysterically as young adolescent kids.

I eventually made my way back down to North 3rd Street where the cookout and drinks were still flowing. The only thing that was different was everyone had a buzz now and the LynchMob girls had crashed the little house party. Most of the LynchMob girls had slept with at least one of the homies besides maybe two of them. And those two were committed to two of the homies after being scooped up. We called it "saving their life". We'd say "you wanna get saved? I'll change ya lifestyle!" and that's what would happen, a baby or two later, your life was changed forever whether the guy who said it meant it and was staying committed forever. That never happened at all. Even with the ones who stayed together, all my homies, every single one of them were cheaters, liars, and snakes.

All my life, I seemed to grow up around snakes and pretty women. Snakes with a vengeance. Real dope dealers. The sad thing was I thought that was normal but when you're doing the devil's work, not staying grounded, not living with the Lord at the forefront of your everyday life, and entertaining foolish thoughts, ideas, and acting on them living out your life daily as if it is the video you just watched on BET or something. You're headed down a dark path, where many never see the light at the end of the other side.

The party was lit. When we finally came through that evening, our grand entrance was always the headline. Being involved with the cities top dogs coming through you'd think the red carpet would've been rolled out because it was at minimum fifteen of us on a day when not everyone came out at the same time. Most days it was straight from the block or Swamp Fox's or a cookout and we would all go purchase new outfit's with hats and sneakers or Timberlands to match everything just to sit in a bar and spill drinks on our shoes or Timb's and allow our clothes to be full of the smell of cigarette smoke and chicken wing grease. That's the life!

This day I felt good. I had so much cash on me along with a pistol and quite a few girls checking me out trying to establish their birthday boy date that was certain to follow at a local motel. Yes, motels were our typical destinations. Thirty bucks in and out.

Tamara couldn't get in the bar. She was way too young looking, and she'd act out if she seen anyone even staring at me. So, I was cool with my girl not getting in, especially with me on the dance floor now, hands all under this woman's sundress, having my way. Wow was this the way all parties would be in an adult environment? It was fun, the attention was like being a star, I guess. The crowd formed a circle screaming, "Go Clabo! It's Ya Birthday!" adding fuel to the fire that was lit since the early afternoon. I fed off that energy and freaked this girl down had her backing it up like Beyoncé does now on stage with Jay. Man, I was having the time of my life until my pistol dropped out of my pocket and cleared the crowd. I quickly recovered it and headed to the front to wipe my sweat that was dripping uncontrollably from my head and got a drink. Instead of water, I got another Heineken and Henny & Coke. All of a sudden after I noticed Sheen in attendance walking through the door, I jumped from my seat hoping his little boy was behind him. Much to my dismay, he wasn't. However, I still went into a zone again. *Was it the brown liquor attacking my body and my mind that was still trying to fully develop? Was I trippin' off the latest Geto Boys and Tupac album?* I know it certainly had an influence on my overall thinking and aspect of life in general. Had me up early lacing up my Nike's. The streets are all I know!

Before long, the bar was shutting down and somehow, I ended up in Doc Boog's black SS dropping him off and being able to take his car for the evening. Not sure why because I had my car. Maybe due to the fact we knew the police never pulled him over because they knew he was valid and straight on all levels. Although he got money, he was looked at by the police as the designated driver for our big homie, ET. They were inseparable. Very seldom did you see one without the other. I was riding the city on the prowl looking for this little weasel as I hit the corner of Priscilla and 4th. A large crowd was gathered on my block! Yep, in front of Swamps Spot. I immediately pulled up, and for the second time today jumped out with a pistol in hand. The only difference was that I was extremely drunk this time. Upon exiting the vehicle, I cocked the gloc 9mm back and started pacing amongst the crowd weaving in and out looking each person up and down. One wrong move or look and I was sure to pull and let go.

The devil had grabbed my mind, corrupted my soul, and the next thing I knew after not seeing the little weasel in sight was that I was in a tussle with Little G. Seems like my mind went blank because all I could remember was my sister laying on top of me and me trying to tell her I couldn't breathe. I must've passed out because I didn't remember anything else.

Several days later, I woke up with tubes in my mouth and not being able to move at all. There was a room full of people around, doctors and all. I looked over with just my eyes cutting back and forth and noticed my mother staring with tears filled in her eyes. I tried to talk but my throat was burning and the tube that was inserted obstructed my vocal cords I assume. Not knowing what had taken place, I did recall a bright light while I was sedated and God telling me, "Son if you continue to play with those guns, I'm going to take you out by a gun. Put them down!!!"

It felt so real and it was stuck in my head. I signaled my hand in the writing motion with hopes somebody in the room would realize I wanted to write something down. Soon my sister says, "He wants a pen and paper." After receiving those items, I scribbled the question, "What happened?" She responded, "You were shot in the stomach. You were drunk and acting up and threatened lil' G and started to raise the gun and he grabbed it. Y'all started wrestling over the pistol and it went off at point-blank range and hit you once in your stomach. You had no pulse; you were life flown to this hospital. The doctors said you were dead, but somehow you came back. You will have to wear a bag on your stomach. You had two surgeries already. You had so many holes in your intestines that they removed some and now that's why you have to poop in a bag that's on your stomach there. You can't see it now. Don't try to move. You have to rest up. The bullet came out your back, so you also have a hole in your back that is draining. The doctor's said you should recover, though."

I pointed to my throat and she assured me that they would be removing the tubes the next morning. I gave the thumbs up and dozed back off. The next time I awoke I saw my homies. My two old heads came to check on me. They sat for a few minutes but was told to come back tomorrow and I would be able to talk then. Visitors seemed to break my sleep way too often. The following day which seemed like forever, the tubes were finally taken out and I was allowed to have ice chips. I had a fresh cut from my chest clear down the middle of my stomach to my hairline down below. They came in and lifted up my gown and started messing around changing the packing that they stuffed in the wound. The doctors told me that they wanted me to get up and start trying to move around. I was nervous, but I was all for it. In my mind, I had a package I had to make something happen with. I had a kid I suddenly became desperate to get my eyes on. So many thoughts had now blanketed my mind. With a little help, I got to my feet and felt so weak as if my legs were going to collapse and my head felt as if it was spinning. I was encouraged to sit back down and take a break before trying again. My insides felt empty. I was bent over trying to ease the pain as best I could. With assistance, I managed to walk up and down the hallway just one time before looking for the bed.

After a few hours of rest, I became restless. Maybe that good medication that was throughout my body had me antsy. I felt the need to get some fresh air though and had high hopes that the next time one of my homeboys stopped past I was going to ask the unthinkable. And sure enough, Doc Boog and ET came walking through the doors. I immediately motioned to help me up and asked let's go for a walk. With a little help, I was up and moving and down the hall, once the nurse unhooked the IV. I mentioned to her that we were going out for some fresh air. She replied, "Alright, take it easy," and motioned towards the wheelchair nearby, suggesting it would be suitable for the long walk. Little did she or my homies know, was that I was about to ask to be driven to the Duke so I could grab my package and get a little something to smoke.

The package was going to be moved by me from my hospital bed. I just needed to make my way to pick it up and sure enough, while my mother sat resting in the room, I was in the passenger seat on the worse ride of my life. Every bump, pothole, and turn jarred my stomach back and forth with great force and excruciating pain. Doc would look over from time to time and ask if I was alright. I knew I had made a huge mistake once again, but there wasn't any turning back. We were almost past Kennywood park when I let out a sigh of pain. Ughh, now I felt pain and nausea at the same time. Besides, I only had on a hospital gown and footies. They passed a blunt back and forth as I grabbed it on the third pass and took a puff thinking that might help the nausea and pain subside. But to my bad judgment, my head felt like it was spinning.

We stopped past Tamara's. She looked surprised and asked what in the world was I doing before cursing uncontrollably as if I had just got caught doing something else. I never got out the car, but once we hit Burns Heights, the speed bumps were enough on my stomach, that I told Doc to pull over and stop. I couldn't take anymore. I was sick as ever. My bag came loose and the smell of *oh my goodness* started to become unbearable. So we were pulling over anyhow, I lifted up my gown and my colostomy bag was filled with a brownish liquid waste. Now I really had to get back. I didn't have a clue on what to do, how to change it or anything, at this point all I could do was to try and hold it in place. I still had to make it to my spot and pick up that package first.

Up in the Heights, I was almost greeted as a celebrity for all the wrong reasons and I didn't need anyone stroking my ego, especially being in this situation. *Why would someone look up to another human being for recovering from a nearly fatal gunshot wound: why were people idolizing that behavior? Was it just the start of a repeated cycle that would go unchecked and become normal for our community? Had the government succeeded in their plan to lock us up within the community? Allow the drug and guns to pour in and wreak havoc? Or was the government even to blame? Had our fathers done their duties and kept a grasp on their families and took the time to teach the children and lead by example, that there was a better way, would we still be headed for self-destruction? Who were all these owners of these bars that littered the community? Why a bar on every corner in a community that barely graduated 60 students in a year? Was this a coincidence that as you headed towards the white neighborhoods, bars became harder to find? Who approved these permits and building plans?*

I began to wonder as I gazed out the window on our way back to the hospital. I'd go into deep thought after I smoked those Philly blunts. Sometimes maybe I overthought, but the feeling was great. Bar after bar, corner after corner, I counted nine bars from the projects to the main road within a three-minute ride through the hood. A flashback of my mother in front of that bar quickly crossed my mind as we sped across one of the many bridges that the city of Pittsburgh is built on. I was sweating even with the window down and air on due to my bag being nearly completely off. One of the longest rides once again.

For the first time in my young life, I couldn't wait to get back to the hospital. I knew I had made a huge mistake by allowing my infatuation for the paper to lead me down a rough road time and time again. This time my selfish ways had my mother crying and cursing me and my homies out when Doc came wheeling me back into the room. Understandably so, we were deserving of every word she said. I managed to climb back into the bed while listening to my mother scorn me and shaking me up by saying the doctors may have to do another procedure because I'm nowhere near healed up and wasn't ready to be in a car with all that movement. And when I was released, they would instruct me to hold a pillow in place over my stomach while I was being transported home.

I spent seventeen days in the hospital under the care of the angels God placed on earth to carry out the work he had called them to do. For the first time since I was eleven years old, I finally sat down and just did absolutely nothing except fiddle with the antenna on the TV trying to get a clear reception. And talking on the house phone, sending pages out and having company. I slept on the couch night after night and day after day. I couldn't eat much because my diet was so strict. I seemed to fall in love with grilled cheese and tomato soup, though. I could eat that for breakfast, lunch, and dinner every day at that time. There were days that I'd try something else and it wouldn't agree with my stomach and decided to come back up! Then there were the days a homie came by to visit and I'd sit on the porch and smoke while my uncle touted for me all day every day. He'd have things rolling all times of the day and night. The power of the mighty dollar. The things I'd do for a stack of dead presidents.

Once my mother caught wind of my dealings at her home, she started searching and threatening that if she ever found anything, it was going down the toilet and a frequent quote from her was, "You haven't learned your lesson yet! If the cops come up in here, they better not find a thing in here and I mean not even one of those stinking cigars you running around smoking!"

Some time passed and my cousin, Twan, stopped through for a visit. I woke up to him standing over me in the living room, dressed in all red saying, "What up, cuz. Who did it?" I started to tell him the story until I noticed the brown handle sticking out of his pocket. I twisted and pulled myself to an upright position, placing my feet on the plastic runner that covered the carpet. "Cuz, chill out. It's all good. Don't worry about it. I'll handle it." Twan was not trying to hear anything I was saying besides who did it and where he was. I then proceeded to tell him the story and told him I was in the wrong. He still wasn't trying to hear what I had to say and even got angry with Reub for not doing something to the little boy himself. Anyone who knew Twan knew that he was not the one to play with or get on his bad side. He was a funny person to be around, but at the same time, the ones who did hang around with him got the blues from time to time and would be sent on assignments… and you better come back with all of your homework done and with your name on it! Very rarely if ever had I heard a story that someone turned in a blank assignment. These boys who wore all red and claimed to be bloods were trained to go to war without any certified combat experience in the US military. But I'm sure that any one of those young men would've been successful and taken in and trusted to be brothers in the war abroad. The problem was they wanted to declare war amongst the folks that looked like them and lived blocks away.

I guess we all acquired that mentality every so often in the neighborhoods we grew up in. We allowed the disharmony of our environment to draw us in and take us down. Just as at the time I was down. Twan pressed on saying he was going to get the little weasel. He was going straight down to where they hung out and was going to handle it. As he headed out the door, I followed behind and was in awe at the red car my cuz was driving. It was all redone. A very flashy Monte Carlo and what looked to be his security. Chunky Len and Diddy Dollars were standing outside the car smoking cigarettes and passing a 40 oz back and forth. We greeted each other and they all jumped in the car to head out.

About half an hour later, my mom's phone was ringing nonstop. Twan had gone down to them boys' hangout spot and jumped out roughing them up, but unable to locate the weasel he was after. But he set the tone, shook them boys down and took whatever they had. I soon after had to intervene and keep the peace amongst Reub and Twan.

Twan wanted to get him because one evening when Twan left Swamps after gambling, he rode down towards the street he had shook them down on and Twan claimed Reub shot at his car. There weren't any holes in his car, just him saying it. But I wasn't going to allow either of them to proceed. I got them both together and squashed that issue before it got to far outta my reach.

I finally sat down long enough to piss my mother off to the point she didn't want any girls visiting me. Tamara lived just around the corner, so I'd just walk to her house if I didn't want to drive after my sister had heard me whining to her about my mom and my mom bickering, fussing about me, she broke down and swapped me out.

My sister had an apartment above the barbershop, which was just about seven houses up from Tamara and a block from my mom's. She gave me the apartment and moved back in with our mom. My nephew D'Juan was just a baby. I babysat him for a couple of hours occasionally. The responsibility just got more real than ever. I couldn't let my sister down and default on that rent payment. I started moving around better after a couple of weeks of bed rest, well couch rest. It seemed as though my ego was now through the roof. I just survived a major gunshot wound, I had an apartment and a really pretty friend on the side I had started seeing. She knew about my girlfriend Tamara, but she was cool with it. She only lived a couple of blocks away. She would have me wait until her parents were in their room for thc night before she gave me the okay to come over and chill. There were days that she'd come over to my new spot above the barbershop, despite the risk of being just a few houses down from Tamara's.

My ego, my thoughts, my ways, my selfishness they were all way out of control. I wanted and demanded to be treated with much respect, but the problem was that I wasn't demonstrating and practicing it in return.

I realized it was time to take my business a step further with a brief talk with my sister and promising her I had given the pistol up for a while and the dream I had with God talking to me. I convinced her to lend me $2500 to advance my business with the promise of paying it back in a few days. She trusted and I delivered. That apartment became everything. The stash spot for weapons, drugs, and cash. I didn't allow much traffic from the homies, but if you had at least 20 dollars you could meet me in the back all night long. I opened up shop and stayed up every night selling poison until the morning light. Then it was time for the other product to start moving. I was the early bird and I always got the worm. I wondered how my customers always had at least $200 every morning. Nothing less than $80 on bad days. If I had the right stamped coin bag, they went like a magician doing a disappearing act. In a blink of an eye, they'd be gone.

Days turned into weeks and weeks into months. My mother started getting my son on the weekends, weekdays, whenever. She had him all the time. She was crazy about her some Quan. She also loved her some Wendy. Wendy was never troubling, loud, or disrespectful. She was always pleasant, understanding, and patient. And to deal with me she had to be very patient and humble.

I seemed to go up and down, round and round with the business. Maybe it was the gambling addiction, the blunt addiction, drinking addiction, or sex addiction. I managed to maintain paying my bills, my car insurance and providing for Quan, making sure he had clean fresh diapers and clothes. I stayed off of Priscilla Ave for a while unless it was to gamble. I had my own little business going, wasn't any need to hit the Ave. I was attempting to keep a low profile and stack my money up. I soon wondered if I was doing too much because it was just a short time later trouble caught back up to me. And this time, it was a double whammy. One after another.

The local police force had started a transition. All the old cops who knew us that sat in the projects, walked the community, knew the community, the children and their parents, and didn't just harass us for no apparent reason, didn't stereotype us either. Mr. Dudley, Mr. Jones, and Mr. Tucker. These officers had almost all retired or were driven out at the same time. The new cops weren't from the neighborhood and didn't live in our community. They came in and immediately started pulling cars over for no reason, jumping out on individuals, groups gathered just being complete jerks with very little regard for a community or the children in it.

There was a cop by the name of Parazeenie that was a total jerk. He would drive by slowly and purposely look and pull his black leather gloves as if to say on behalf of OJ and his case, this is payback. We soon gave him the nickname Superman and RoboCop. He caught me slippin' one day as I was just walking home from my mom's just a block away. I had just cut up a half-ounce of dubs and put them in the medicine bottle. It was almost like he had sat at the top of the hill from my mom's and was waiting for me to come back out. As soon as I hit the corner adjacent to Andy's Bar, the cop pulled up in a marked car and rolled the window down screaming, "Hey you. Clabo. Stop right there. Don't move." Before throwing the patrol car into park with a heavy jerk of the car and the sound of the door opening, I turned to run away. The only problem was that I wasn't in any position to run I was still nurturing a healing wound and had a colostomy bag attached to my stomach. One thing for sure though, was that I wasn't getting caught with this medicine bottle on me. I reached into my flannel pocket and launched the bottle as far as I could before he wrestled me to the ground. It turned into a messy situation and I felt pain all over. I screamed, cursed, and acted in a volatile manner because of the harassment that was occurring. My bag had come off which left poop on my clothes and my intestines unprotected with the chance of getting infected. Blood was seeping out from underneath my shirt. I just felt the warm flow with what seemed like a steady stream. This cop didn't care that a crowd had gathered and were screaming obscenities directly towards him. He had me cuffed and placed at the rear of his vehicle with a backup patrolman watching me. He had his flashlight on and was walking back and forth slowly saying he'd find it; he saw me throw something. I prayed and hoped that he didn't find it. I knew I had a chance because the grass and weeds to the vacant home were way overgrown. Due to the overpaid inspectors and city workers that performed minimum work daily. Usually, I'd see the big red 2500 trucks with two guys who looked as if they drank soon after, before, and during work.

Within five minutes of prayers and many scenarios racing through my head, Robocop says, "Bingo! Put him in the car. He's going downtown tonight!" Now, here I am looking out the backseat of another police car. This time I was headed to the big house, the Allegheny County Jail. As the police cruiser pulled away, I sat in disbelief. *Was this really happening? All I was trying to do was get to my girlfriend's house. I wasn't causing trouble or anything. What would happen with my bag that was caught onto my belt buckle? This cop had me in his car smelling like this?*

The police station was just less than two minutes away. We were only on Third street. He only has to turn onto north second at the top of the hill and hang a left turn, then a right. *Would I be able to call my mom's house phone? Would I even get a call? What's happening to my life? Would I have to sit in jail long before I could get bonded out?* Every thought flashed repeatedly across my mind one after another. Here I am riding in the back seat past my girlfriend's house as she just looked on from the porch making eye contact with me with a look that said, "I told you."

We made it to the station. Robocop tried asking a question, but I just ignored him and asked one request: when do I get to make a phone call so I can make sure I get bonded up out of this hell hole? This jerk responded with a, "You may not get a call." I immediately started swearing and cursed him out and even threw in a couple of indirect threats.

After sitting in a cold holding cell for three hours while patrolmen came in and out with one particular individual, I recognized Mr. Yurbie. Mr. Yurbie was drunk. falling all over the place and saying really off the wall stuff. Continually taking the palm of his hand and smacking himself in the mouth. My gosh, that had to hurt with the force he applied each time rocking back and forth. Just when I attempted to block Yurbie out of my mind while lying on the cold hard bench with my eyes closed dozing off, a loud voice, clicking of handcuffs, and the sound of keys jingling brought me back to my senses and I sat upright. Robocop was saying, "Let's go. On your feet. Put your hands behind your back and step back." *Alright. Here it is.* For once I wanted to be placed in handcuffs. The reason being was I felt as though the sooner I got downtown and processed was the sooner I could see a judge and get bonded out.

Here I am several years later in the back of the Duquesne police cruiser on a ride to jail, not a juvenile facility this time. I had heard many stories of how dirty and filthy and all the corrupt guards that the county jail was known for. But now I was going to experience it firsthand. It didn't seem to be too good of a deal as it's turning out to look like. I wasn't prepared for this day. I didn't have attorney's fees or much bond money if it was more than five thousand dollars and that five thousand would've made me flat broke if the judge set it at that amount. I Guess I was sure to find out shortly. As we had just pulled up downtown in the rear lower level of this huge red brick building with tiny windows over ten stories high. The Allegheny County Jail.

The cruiser sat idle momentarily until the gate slowly opened. Now my heart rate was going. I could feel my hands getting sweaty as well as my underarms, the sweat bead dripping down my rib cage. I had gotten cotton mouth all of a sudden. Man, they said this jail was dirty, but I'm dirty. I smell like poop. I hope my wound and stomach don't get infected. I prayed out to God in my head. But through it all I never let the cop see me sweat or look worried. At least I thought I didn't.

To my disbelief and total surprise, one of the very first guards I noticed and made eye contact with was Mr. Little, my homies older cousin. He stood 6 foot 4 inches tall with big burly shoulders. He had his shirt folded up over his huge arms. I remember being at the party back in 1985 as a little kid, the Taylor family had for his NFL draft day party to the Miami Dolphins. He recognized me and said "Chafe. What's up? I got you." *Thank you, Jesus.* My prayers were answered just that fast. All I wanted was a couple of phone calls and that's exactly what I got! Also, new linen and a bright crispy red outfit with Allegheny County Jail stamped in white letters on the back of the shirt. He expedited my paperwork also because I got processed so fast while others sat still in a holding tank that looked hot and funky with drug addicts; white, black, young, and old. I did notice one guy in particular as I stood outside the tank making my call. He was just on the news the night before for a triple homicide. He shot up a vehicle with an assault weapon. Mr. Little allowed me to shower up and offered to throw my clothes away. I agreed. To my surprise, a nurse showed up and cleaned my wound and had new bags for me. She was so nice that she even waited and put it on for me.

I was up for a bond hearing and received an O/R (Own Recognizance). I believe it was because I filled all the relevant information out correctly, honestly, and to the best of my ability not leaving any question unanswered, not one blank line was left on the paper. Most importantly, I believe that I had an address with several references.

I still managed to sleep upstairs on the sixth floor on E block. I didn't understand that since I was going home, and I wasn't charged with killing anyone. I didn't quite understand that part, but I was happy when that door popped open and the guard said, "Chafe. Pack it up."

Chapter Eleven

What You Gon' Do?

We knew who it was before the vehicle even hit the corner because she played the same song over and over. Bone Thugs and Harmony. Yes, it was at the top of the billboard charts in 1996. However, we laughed so hard as this light-skinned tall young lady with jet black silky hair that hung so far down her back. She drove slowly past the Ave with her sunglasses on sitting pretty in a GMC Blazer with the subwoofer speakers rattling houses. Something was a little different this time though because she looked hard in me and Pinhead's direction before coming to a complete stop and yelling "What's up? Come here, Clabo." I looked and started approaching asking, "What's up?" I didn't think she wanted any of this business I had on me, so what was it that she wanted? She calmly and with total surprise to me, she says, "What's up? I want you to come and visit me later." The element of surprise is something else. I said to her, "Don't you mess with CY?" Yes, I knew they had something going. She also knew I had pistol-whipped him some time ago and I'm sure she knew he would feel some kind of way if he knew what she was trying to do. The problem was I had squashed that issue.

I apologized and allowed him to start coming around without worrying if I was going to do something to him again. I was past that stage, though. We were cordial at this point. But this fine young lady, well Gina wasn't quite that young. She was older than me by a couple of years. But she was definitely a ten!

I allowed my lust and the temptations to take over and things happened. Everyone knew, but everyone also knew not to say anything to me about it. I cut it out soon after I realized that he was infatuated with that girl and knowing I didn't want her long term either. Just a little fun in the sun for a short term. She was using me to make him jealous and as soon as I used my right head and realized her motives, I put a stop to it.

I was slowly learning to stand for something, or I'd fall for anything, every time. There was a message and a blessing afterward. CY ended up having a kid with her. So that was the blessing I was blocking for them both.

Tamara and I were on and off. On when I wanted and off when I felt like it. This was a pattern that soon became almost normal for me. *Was I that out of touch with what life was about when it came to respecting and being honest with my "girlfriend" and myself? If I wasn't going to be faithful, why wouldn't I just let her go on to live her life?* I had already had a child with a woman I wasn't committed to and here I was repeating the same thing. I began to question my disheartened tone of voice. I wasn't very outspoken. I was quiet and my inner thoughts were always one thing, but my actions showed otherwise. Why was my mind playing tricks on me? Had I already lost my mind? Was I born with an undiagnosed condition? Most of my friends agreed that something was missing. Was I that little skinny boy from a small city in the heart of the plagued steel mill town of Duquesne, PA that would never be heard of? Why was I idolizing and following after the same guys that would probably sell my mother the potentially lethal dose of narcotics? Would the Lord guide me and save me? I needed a breakthrough and I needed it right now.

Back Again

After a few weeks passed from the day I bonded out, I found myself face to face once again with Robocop. This time he pulled up on me while I was getting on my motorcycle in front of Andy's Bar. It was almost the exact spot where the last encounter happened. The scenario was just a little different. I had just started the bike up. Hoochie Dog was jumping on the back 'cause he had asked for a ride up the street to his home. Neither of us had helmets on and we were both in possession of contraband. Going back to jail for the contraband wasn't an option. So as Robocop hurried to slam his patrol car into park. I yelled out for Hoochie Dog to hold on. With a laugh and an "oh shhhiiii…" he dropped the two 40 oz bottles he had in the bag ready to go. I gunned the throttle changing gears as if I was Freddie Spencer or Kenny Roberts. With the officer in hot pursuit and neither of us wearing any protective gear or anything else, our lives were certainly on the line. Hoochie Dog laughed but hollered, "Let me off when we hit the next corner!" I had no plan to stop until I knew we both had time to get off and flee without getting caught. At the beginning of the chase, I didn't have a getaway plan. I was just running and gunning the bike. As I slowed down on top of Grant Street to make the left onto Seventh street, the police car almost hit my back tire before I could get the bike back into first gear for a quick take off. I'm sure he would have been ecstatic had he been able to hit us and make us fly off the bike for probably a near-death or fatal injury. I heard more sirens and noticed another patrol car ahead blocking the next intersection as I zoomed in and out near the rear of the car as it sat in the street. I begin to shake but kept my composure as they started to lose ground on us. But my next move soon approached as I was still going at a very high rate of speed in fourth gear up this hill that the cemetery was on where we played our Thanksgiving Day turkey bowl games. The hill went almost straight up with a steep slope straight back down once you hit the peak at the top. I hadn't quite thought that through when I decided to go up the hill, flying nonstop.

We hit the top of that hill and were literally off the ground as if I was attempting a stunt. It happened so fast. Hoochie Dog was screaming, "OH SNAP DOG WE GON' DIE! HOLD ON!" as we soared through the air. We had to have been high enough in the air to clear a vehicle if it was on the other side of the peak. When the bike landed to my surprise and blessing, we landed on both tires and continued. I was shaking uncontrollably as we had now lost sight of any police lights. I kept moving and ended up behind Burns Heights where I turned the engine off, killed the lights, and cruised to a resting stop before we jumped off. I laid the bike down in some bushes along the fence that separated the projects from the nice houses. I'll never forget how bad I was shaking when I got off that black and red Ninja with the 750 cc.

Once again, God had saved my life, kept me for another day after I made yet another terrible choice to flee the harassing officer. I wondered if I'd have a warrant now that he had seen my face? I'd soon find out because I wasn't going to hide for long after the evening was over.

A few days later, I received a summons in the mail and ended up hiring a lawyer to represent me. Now I had to pay Mark Lancaster for this case, also. What was I getting myself into? Things were spiraling out of control. At that time, I had no idea that I was labeled by the cops as a highly aggressive, gun-toting thug. I liked the title as a thug in the streets, but not from the police. In one of his interviews, Tupac said he was a thug and enjoyed the thug life so that was what I wanted to do, be a thug and dish out slugs and mean mugs.

I had settled down a bit from that as I was still recovering from a self-inflicted wound of sorts. And I had kept the memory of the message God had said to me about living and or dying by the gun. Every day was a constant battle to evade the cops now. Every day brought the unknown. Would this be the last time I walked out of my mom's door or the last time I'd hug her or hear her cry out to the Lord to watch over her defiant child and to protect me as I continued with the reckless everyday behavior? Who would have ever thought or imagined seeing someone shoot at the authorities? Were they there to protect and serve or were they the enemies of the people? I sure felt as if they were the enemies of the people once I was harassed this time.

Get That Heat Up Off You

The same bar we got chased from a week prior, I had just walked down to from Tamara's to pick up our food and was standing near the pool tables waiting on my food order. I stood and watched as ET was knocking ball after ball in with a little grin on his face. This guy had only one eye but was the *best* pool player I had ever seen. He was even better under the influence of the Hennessey that he loved to sip on. I watched as he beat my older cousin, Mike Stock, and then beat Bowie City twice. Here I am, sitting around the with fellas who were all old enough to be drinking here at the bar when Robocop walks in with his partner behind him. *Here we go again!* The only problem was I had no place to run to. He walked straight toward me with his black gloves on pulling them tight for no reason except for intimidation purposes. He walks up to me and says, "You're underage and under arrest for being in here." Everyone in the bar erupted in yells and unkind words as he just proceeded to forcefully handcuff and search me. I didn't have time to even throw the bag of business I had in my pocket. Right in front of everyone, he pulled out the bag and smiled. Here I am back to the Allegheny County Jail. This time, I had to make bail.

I had to pay one thousand six hundred and forty dollars. My little funds had dwindled right before my eyes within two months. I had less than five hundred dollars in cash, less than three hundred in product, two pending drug cases along with a child to raise and another surgery still yet to reverse my intestines and close up my stomach. I realized Robocop was targeting me and I couldn't afford to get caught again. So, I reeled in a couple extra 'touters' to bring the customers to me instead of me standing around waiting on them. I was on a mission. I had lawyer fees; rent was due, and Wendy needed pampers and milk for our child.

Getting a job never seemed to cross my mind. I needed money, and I needed it quick and in a hurry. I was totally out of the product I sold now, and it went dry, a "drought" as we called it, for about a week. In between that time, I only had the coin bags for sale, but I had made a bad choice one evening trying to make a come up off of gambling and ended up losing more than I could swallow.

For the first time, stress, panic, and desperation set in. To my surprise, somebody had taken notice and must've seen and heard the desperation and struggle. As I came to ET to spend my very last three hundred dollars, he asked if that was all I had. I said yes and told him I would be alright; I just had to grind harder. He told me not to worry. He told me he had just bought two Eagles. The next thing he said was for me to save my three hundred. He instructed me to put it up and that he would be right back. He jumped in the passenger seat with Doc Boog driving and they pulled off. Half an hour later, they pulled back up in front of my mom's house where I was sitting on the porch. They got out and sat on the steps. ET went on to tell me he was giving me four and a half ounces of fish scales and that he was charging me the price he got it for and that I could flip it a couple of times just to pay him back when I got myself back right. But it also came with the agreement that I wouldn't gamble anymore and that he wanted me to give my attorney one thousand dollars every flip.

The game was on! This was the break I needed. I took most of it to the stove with the help of the chemist and VOILA!!! Just like that, that easy 4 ½ ounces turned into something that made me smile and go harder. I had made my mind up that I had to let the apartment go so I could focus on finding my rhythm. I had the pressure on despite being told that I had time to find myself, focus and do what I had to do.

ET must've had faith and trust in me, so in return, I would make sure to get his money before anything. I wasn't going to take his kindness for weakness or lightly at *all*! Now that I had gained trust from him, I could probably get a lot more if I needed him again someday. But right now, I had to get his money back to him. That wasn't a problem or an issue whatsoever! I stayed up almost all night every night, and during the day I'd sit in front of the gambling spot instead of going into the gambling spot and hustled there. I got a little smarter, though. I'd have my stash across the street from me in-sight, but far enough that the cops couldn't put it on me if they happened to find anything. I never brought out more than two hundred and fifty worth at a time. I learned so fast now that I had to save hundreds first for the thousands to accumulate. Almost like the saying you have to crawl before you walk!

At this point, I was crawling quickly. On a bad day, three or four hundred was getting folded and tucked in. A good day, I'd sell small weight and my usual street business and would clear at least twelve hundred dollars. Finally, I was seeing something. But as soon as I saw it, it was going right back out to my attorney Mr. Lancaster. Once he was paid off for both cases, I felt a little relief, especially once ET, Boog, and I drove into downtown Pittsburgh to make the last payment and allowed them to hear and ask the questions I didn't think or know to ask the attorney myself. Lancaster assured us that he was preparing for trial and felt good about it all. Now with the lawyer fees taken care of and the big homie paid off, I had seven thousand dollars and still eight weeks before trial.

ET had my loyalty, my word, my bond, and assertion that I would always ride for my big homie no matter the circumstance. Big homie helped me, guided me, and saved me just as I asked God to do for me just a short time ago. God delivered. He's real! I know he is. We converse all the time and he seem to always answer me. He told me to put the pistols down. I did and the gunplay stopped just as fast as I started it. Some of the things we got ourselves into, all I could do was ask God to bless and watch out for us all. I'd do or be involved with something I knew wasn't right and still pray before and after it was done. *What was wrong with me? God said not to play with pistols, or He'd take me out that way. But he didn't say not to incorporate some other little homies that would!*

The message was clear. What was I hearing? What message was I grasping? Or was I even trying to hear any of it at all? Here I am, nineteen years old, rolling with some OGs that took turns stacking stacks. And when we had a customer, we had them for life.

I started to get paid and wanted to flex. My other old head Bowie City had just got home from doing a few months on a state parole violation and jumped right back into getting money. He still had Tamara's mother wrapped around his finger but was a little bitter at the fact that she got caught in a bust with Juice from Clairton. It probably could've happened anywhere else, and he would not have cared. But because it was someone from Clairton, that made it that much worse.

Tamara and I started to become on and off again. I was mainly focused on getting money nowadays and I wasn't ready for the commitment of a serious relationship.

I had met this nice-looking chick one day as she was walking through the Avenue. I caught her peeking at me right before she stopped and asked if I had some smoke. "Absolutely I do!" She had just invited herself to a seat on the steps of the gambling spot. She had a skirt on, as I noticed tattoo prints going up her leg. She instantly had my attention, so I proceeded on with the small talk. She told me her name was Ke-Ke and told me she had just moved to the city. We smoked, exchanged numbers, and carried on with our day. Later that evening she called me and asked if I'd stop by her place and smoke. I accepted the invitation and things went pretty well. I'll just say I stayed a lot longer than I expected to. She was cool. She liked what I liked at the time and we clicked instantly. She was also hood and knew all the hood homies from H-Town Crippin' I found that out one day when I stopped up her house because she said somebody wanted to holler at me.

I went upstairs, opened the door and it was like six homies with blue on smoking and looking like straight gangstas. Oh, they were. I recognized a couple of 'em and had heard their names. I heard all about the work they were putting in and I'm sure they heard about me, also. We saw one another before when their old head TC would meet my old heads ET and Doc Boog. We talked, smoked a little bit and exchanged numbers. It was on from there.

We kept in touch on a few different subjects. I now had another avenue to distribute or acquire everything. I had to try and spread my wings as best as I could. Ke-Ke knew I had a girlfriend and saw other women.

My mother started seeing too much. Although I wasn't staying there very often, I would still be in and out. She got tired of it and yelled all the time, so I got with Bowie City and we went half on a two-bedroom apartment. Up until this point, I was disciplined on how I spent every dollar, especially being I had a court date that was fast approaching now. I would've preferred to wait until after my court date to make any moves like that, but for the business, it was a strategic move being it was just across the street from Burns Heights.

I blended with anyone I felt like blending with when I was ready to. My daily routine started to slightly change. I invested in some Frank White and things started taking off tremendously. Before noon, I'd be rid of at least 200-coin bags each day. The day before my court hearing, I counted out eleven thousand dollars and put that in ET's hand to hold just in case I didn't come back home the following day. Trusting him with that wasn't an issue at all.

We all decided to go out the night before my hearing, to celebrate me parting ways I assumed. We bar hopped on a Wednesday fall night in November. Somehow, we ended up in East Liberty at a popular bar called The Name of the Game. We were twelve deep - four deep in three different vehicles. We pulled up to a packed parking lot and headed inside. I had paid forty dollars to get past the security being that I wasn't of age only to leave right back out in less than twenty minutes.

As we were walking back out going to our vehicles, a group of young ladies was following behind us taking notice. A woman's voice could be heard yelling out, “Hey you in the ponytail, come here.” We all looked as the light-skinned young lady was now heading towards us. The homies started laughing and saying, “She wants you, Clabo.” So I took heed being that I knew I was the only one with a ponytail. I had taken my braids out the day before in preparation for my hearing thinking the thug look with the braids would have the judge stereotyping me.

We walked up to one another and instantly I noticed the pretty face and exotic eyes on this woman. We talked quickly as she had jotted her phone number down on a piece of paper with the name Monica on it. I told her I had a court hearing in the morning and I very well may be going to prison, but I assured her that if I didn’t go to jail that I would call her. I walked away with the biggest smile on my face and carefully placed Monica’s phone number in my little pocket on the front side of my Karl Kani jeans.

For some reason, that night, I laid in my bed and played that moment of her calling me out over and over in my head. It was something in this woman’s eyes that stuck with me all night. The following morning, I went to my mother’s and asked her for a ride into town. She ended up parking and coming along. Mr. Lancaster was in the hall near the courtroom entrance talking with what looked like a prosecutor or somebody. My mother and I stood at a short distance until we were signaled and called upon after they had finished their conversation. Mr. Lancaster waived us over, briefly speaking, then instructing us to follow him inside.

Once we got inside, it was very busy with attorneys, defendants, and spectators. I stood next to my attorney as my mother took a seat. Lancaster looked over and smiled. He said something really quick in legal language that I wasn't familiar with, then he nudged me and said say, "Yes sir!" He then said, "Alright. We will sign these papers and you're good to go. It's done. The prosecutor agreed they didn't have a strong enough case on either of the charges." I looked like "really?!?"

Wow, it's over. Lancaster is a beast! He explained that the cop didn't follow protocol and that he was a rookie. He told me to steer clear of that officer because he had it out for me and that the officer Robocop was very upset with the outcome, and that the officer would learn the correct method of what it took to get a proper arrest and conviction. I thanked him, shook his hand, and hugged him before getting the heck up out of that courthouse.

I stepped back outside and screamed, "Hallelujah!" before giving my mother another huge bear hug.

Chapter Twelve

Go Get It

Back in the hood, I hit Tamara's and played around a little bit, letting her know I wasn't going anywhere just yet and asked her to go get some charcoal because we were firing up the grill. It was back to business as usual. I got back to our apartment and kicked it with Bowie City for a few minutes before his friend Tracy knocked on the door. CY came knocking right behind her to see what was up with me, saying he heard I beat the case. We all started hanging out with ET and Doc Boog as well as Bowie City and the rest of the homies: Tone B, Flash, Rooski, R-Dog, Speedy John, Sweet Pea, Rick, Pinhead, the Dirty Pimp, and many more. Larry Luv, Seer, Crump and the list could go on and on. We slowly took over the city. I continued seeing Ke-Ke. She wanted more of a consistent relationship, but I was more on a casual do what I want friendship. I wasn't sure how much longer that would last, but either way, I was alright with it. I had taken a liking to Monica as our conversations evolved. She could hold a very good conversation on the phone, and we started communicating more and more daily. We soon realized that she knew my cousins' Tee, Twan, and Rookie. I got the 411 about her from

Twan - that was a two-way street, though. Twan was real. He didn't care who you were or what walk of life you came from.

I saw him one evening at the Sportsmen's Bar just up the street from our apartment and I asked him about Monica. He said, "Yes, she's a good girl. She is about her business, gets money, and don't be messing with a lot of people. She's a woman that had the same boyfriend for years. She's good peoples." He then said, "But she's not good for you! That's my girl and you'll do her wrong!" He went on to say that the next time he saw her that he was going to tell her not to mess with me. And sure enough, he did just that. She didn't listen.

We laughed it off and continued talking. I explained that I had a young girl, but she wasn't quite on my level. That she was a bit immature and liked to cause drama. Monica said she wasn't scared, and it showed by the way she started coming around, traveling clear across the city to see me. She'd bring a couple of her friends along and CY was usually the one I happened to be plugging in with one of them. I, however, didn't disclose any of the other women I had known or hung out with. *Was I wrong for not mentioning that?* If I planned on a long-term friendship with her, I probably should have. *A long-term friendship though? I was living day to day doing as I pleased. Why would I want to change that?*

Payback Time

After winning the state championship and getting D-1 offers and a scholarship to Duquesne University in Pittsburgh, PA, Crump went on to play college basketball and in his sophomore year, we decided to all attend the backyard brawl at the Civic Arena. The Pitt Panthers were playing against the Duquesne Dukes. We all sat mid-level on the same side and watched as Crump put on a clinic in the first half along with great shooting from beyond the three-point mark from Mike James. We were tuned in to the game when two guys with orange sweatshirts on caught my attention clear on the opposite side of the arena. *Oh no. It can't be him. No, it isn't. Yes, it is him!* My blood began to boil, and my heart rate increased dramatically. I leaned over to ET sitting next to me "Yo, there's that bully from Clairton that got out on me at the Hollywood Club a while ago! That's him over there!" ET told me to chill out. "Don't look. Act like we don't see him." It was difficult for me to watch any more of the game without focusing and keeping my eyes on those orange shirts. He had to know we were going to be at the game to support Crump. What was he thinking? Or did he think he was that tough? We were about to find out because the plan was at half time, we would walk to their side if they got up for the concession stand and see if the element of surprise could be applied. And sure enough, with less than one minute left before the half ended, the orange shirts could be seen walking from the back. We waited until they were up and out of sight then we all jumped up and hurried off to the other side wherc they should've been at by now.

The plan sure came together because as we walked up to them, they didn't have a clue. They were ordering food. Attorney D. Shrager had noticed ET and was about to say something to him when ET put his index finger up to his lips signaling the shush be quiet gesture before tapping the bully on the shoulder. The bully turned around with nachos in his hand and ET cocked back and sucker-punched him dead square in the jaw causing the bully to stumble back and drop his food. Then ET proceeded to punch him two more times. Now it was time to make him pay big time. Ole boy then ran up to him with a razor blade and slit the bully's throat from ear to ear. Blood started squirting everywhere and everyone who was in the line at the concession stand started screaming in a panic.

We all took off for the exits and got into our vehicles just as the Pittsburgh police cars started swarming the scene along with EMTs. Someone took notice that Bowie City and Speedy John didn't run out with us. Bowie City acted as if he wasn't with us, they said. That was a move he'd wish he hadn't done because he was arrested and booked on attempted homicide charges and had his mugshot placed on the 11 o'clock news.

When he eventually got bonded out, he seemed to have an attitude as if I was wrong or as if it was my fault. It wasn't my fault at all. Only God could judge me. For some reason, things started to change. He had always made his way wanting to be different, to have different coin bags, and other things. We all still hung together, but you could feel and notice something was just a little different concerning him. I didn't quite understand his reasoning, but that was his choice. He decided to act as if he wasn't with us and that's how he got caught.

Speedy John got caught also, but he didn't complain, cry, or get an attitude. He laughed it off, as usual, made jokes about it, and moved on. Speedy John took a couple for the homies from time to time.

What You Think

I also didn't understand why I had to wait and buy packages off Bowie City when he had the Frank White moving. We were roommates and his connect, Nitty, told him several times to let me eat the same way he let Bowie eat instead of making me pay the price that everyone else was charged. For about nine months straight, while the Frank White was on the block, nothing else moved until that was gone. Everyone in every city wanted it from Pittsburgh to Philadelphia where it was being made at. Nitty would come to our apartment at the oddest times in the middle of the night and conduct business with Bowie. Either he was picking up money to go out of town to re-up or he was picking up Bowie to ride with him. Sometimes he just came to smoke and chill out.

A lot of people feared Nitty. Maybe because he was known to be sneaky and a little throwed off. He was known to put work in and had money.

I remember one night he pulled up at our apartment at 3:30 am and woke me up with the car pulling up in the alley where my bedroom window faced. I jumped up, grabbed my pistol, and woke up Bowie. Nitty had a tech 9 in his hand and was wearing swimming shoes. Bowie opened the door while I stood at the top of the steps with my pistol clutched in my hand. I heard Bowie asking, "What up, Dog?" Nitty replied, "What's up. Let smoke something and chill out. Put the news on. I just spanked ole boy." I woke up real quick like "what?" I put my pants and shoes on and proceeded down the steps and greeted this lunatic. He said, "What up young buck. Roll this up," and threw a big bag of greens on the table next to the tech 9 that he had sitting there. Bowie scanned the channels and tuned in to breaking news live.

Nitty then asked Bowie, "What up, Dog? Are you letting him eat?" Then he asked me if Bowie was letting me eat before Bowie could answer him, I just said, "Yeah, it's cool," and left it like that as Bowie just looked on at the TV. That second there I knew it was time to make a change.

I kept my composure, maintained buying six every two days until I was talking business one day with Monica. She let me know that her uncle from the Northside was trying to get on! As we conversed, she asked why I kept buying off Bowie instead of just taking a ride up to Philly where I knew the business was at and get on myself? I named a few reasons why not. Needed a rental car; needed a designated driver; and didn't know the exact area. She offered to get the rental car and said she'd be the designated driver. So I said, "Alright, I'm with that."

We'd just find where we needed to be when we got there. We'd rent a hotel room and get a local newspaper to read it and see where the most crime was happening. Then we'd ask a few questions with people in general conversation while we were out. We'd ask our waitress; whomever.

Now we had a plan! I have a rider. She's a straight-up and down thorough chick just like my cousin Twan said! She's a keeper. Something about this Monica had gained more and more attention and my time. I slowly found myself spending more time with her throughout the week. She had an apartment on the west side of Pittsburgh in a nice neighborhood. Neighbors like something I had never experienced before. And I liked it because I could and would do my dirt in the Duke and throughout the city every day, then go to my safe haven in the evenings on a one-way street; a secluded area where nobody knew me. I didn't bring anyone over there at all. I didn't trust anyone at all like that at the time.

I'd come back to the apartment that Bowie and I shared every day just to hustle, change clothes, and chill out during the day. I was still seeing Tamara occasionally during the day, as well as Ke-Ke. She was getting addicted to me, but I couldn't deliver as needed. She already had a child and I felt as though I couldn't take that all on at the time, so I somewhat let her go off, OFF on a date with Bowie my sort of like, still my roommate although I rarely if ever laid my head there again. She told me that she called me one night on the house phone we had and was looking for me and Bowie answered the phone and went and picked her up and took her to the hospital with her son due to him being sick. She also told me that he was saying, "Forget Clabo. Leave him alone. He has a woman," and so on. I simply told her that it was cool, and that Bowie was just jealous of my life. And that it's alright he's mad because I didn't need him anymore and wasn't spending my money with him anymore. This is why I say all my life I grew up around snakes and pretty women. But ultimately, I ended the conversation by telling her she could date him, and I didn't care because I couldn't give her the time she wanted.

We left things off like that and occasionally I'd call her and catch up on old times and the latest vibes with him and all. We remained good friends. Her cousin was messing with CY, so I'd run across her sometimes and knew everything that was happening. She let me know that Bowie was pissed at me because when Monica and I went to Philly the first time to meet a connect, I allowed my cousin Reub and CY to come along. When we would get back every 4 to 5 days on purpose I would go to the apartment and split our business up at the kitchen table while he was probably upstairs with Ke-Ke, laying up or whatever. And he instantly had lost customers, because our product was top notch.

Chicago and Red Bull started making lots of noise in the streets and we lowered our prices by fifty dollars. That wasn't a loss at all being that we now got extras! Yes, every bundle in Pittsburgh was ten-coin bags, but up in Philly, every bundle was thirteen-coin bags which meant we got extra bags per bundle. When you start adding those three extras up when you're buying a couple of hundred bundles, you now talking about thousands and thousands of dollars in extras alone. This became a major game-changer.

We all started blowing up so quick. Reub had down bottom, all the young boys on their strip. CY and I had everything else. CY wouldn't invest too much. Instead of doubling up on the flip, he played safe every flip putting the same amount up. Reub and I were all in every time and it showed. We both bought new cars. I bought my mother a new car, also. I'll never forget the day I told her to let's go car shopping and that she could pick out whatever she wanted. She looked like, "What? No. No, I'm not!" I told her I wanted to do this because her car was old, and she needed one. I knew that I had contributed to tearing it up years ago when I'd drift it down the street and always forgot to put gas in it or move the seat back into her position. She finally agreed! And that moment was priceless! I finally felt my accomplishments paying off! Yes, here I am praising my dirty work, glorifying stacks of cash that the one decision years ago I made to stick my hand on the burning stove. I knew the stove was hot but continued touching it over and over again. Being infatuated with the power and money from the streets the poison was bringing me, blinded me every day after moving forward.

Snakes in The Grass

With more money, more problems arose; mostly due to my poor decision making. Now a decision had to be made. Bowie City got robbed for his whole package that he had just got in, but I wasn't made aware of that happening from him. He didn't call me or mention to me that this had happened at all. I found this out from Monica! *How did Monica know this before me? Or before anyone else in the hood?* Well simply because Bowie City once again was running his mouth to some female telling her that he had thought I robbed him, and he was planning to kill me the next time he had the opportunity to do so!

So now I'm faced with a huge decision. Do I just kill him first? Or do I simply confront him with what I had heard? Only time would tell as I contemplated my next move. But in the meantime, one thing for certain, two things for sure - I wasn't going anywhere! If anything, I was ego-driven now and curious to confront the situation. Nobody threatens me!

I let my cousin Reub and CY know and asked for their advice. I'll just say that they saved his life. However, in-between time, I would pop up at the darnedest times of day and night ready, almost trying to provoke him. I brought people around every day; started meeting customers there and being disrespectful.

Now that the tables had turned. I was up. My money was growing. My business was booming. Pockets were bulging all day every day! His customers were now MY customers and I would meet them right in front of him! Had I not heard about his ill intentions,

I would have offered to let him borrow money and offered to find out who had robbed him.

It soon became the word on the streets that I was mad about Ke-Ke and had him robbed. Maybe it was just his conscience getting the best of him because he was a snake in the grass and felt the bad vibe I deliberately was now inflicting. I was by no means upset about a woman. I had already approved, signed, and sealed the deal firsthand with her without his knowledge. He wasn't man enough to tell me what he was doing, though. Who was this guy that I had moved in with?

Turned out to be a valuable lesson learned though. Keep an eye on your enemy. Never trust anyone in these streets. There may come a point in the game that you might have to put your supposed friend down in the ground someday. The very same person you looked up to as a big brother, a paragon!

Oh, You Gangsta

Not only was I deep inside the game, but I was also about to become a father to another child! Tamara said she was nearly six months pregnant and although we weren't seeing each other very often, I knew it was probably mine because she was still madly in puppy love with me. Being the arrogant, hot-headed, selfish kid I was, I denied that it was my child, partially so I could buy time with Monica because she was the woman that I could see spending the rest of my life with, despite how much she had investigated me, stalked me, and went through my phone while I was drunk sleep! One thing I knew and felt in my heart was that I could certainly trust her with my life; she had already saved my life by giving me valuable information one day before a snake bit me. She was definitely about me and only me every day. She wasn't around for the money, as she had helped get me to where I was financially. She was a team Clabo player, my biggest cheerleader, my best fan, and was always on point. Something was just different on many levels. She wasn't like any of the girls I had met. I felt as though she would never violate the code.

The bond we were forming was authentic. And she promised that if the child was mine, that she would comfort and love the baby as if it was hers. And she meant it because the baby girl came out looking like my twin. There wasn't any denying that gorgeous little girl that was nearly named after me. She was certainly mine. I took the responsibility on immediately and loved Naizah with my whole heart. She wasn't my first child, but she was certainly my first daughter. We still had agreed to take a paternity test and then Tamara said she would be walking me downstairs after the results to sue me for child support as she was bitter, very angry, and wanted to use the government for housing and care as well. That was all good. We went for support. I paid faithfully and got my child faithfully. Also, Quan and Naizah spent plenty of time with Monica and I. Probably more with Monica because I was still running the streets constantly. And we had managed to be blessed with a gift of our own that we went half on.

We put enough work in together and she soon developed a baby bump of her own! Here I am about to have a third child by the time I'm 21. Naizah was only four months old and we were expecting our first child in seven months. I certainly was digging myself in a hole. Was I setting myself up for failure?

Chapter Thirteen

Step Ya Game Up

It was time for me to step my game up. Money was coming in fast, faster than I had even imagined. Along the way, we acquired two more connects. We went to pick up a package one day and Poppi had gone back to Santo Domingo per the conversation we had with Junior and KeKo. They assured us he would be back the following week, but both of these guys slipped me their number while the other wasn't looking and told me I could call them to get whatever I wanted whenever, and that their business would be just as good. It would just have a different name on it. I was fine with that. That way, I would never run out. They were desperate for the business and money to the point they offered to lower the price and start bringing it to Pittsburgh for us. So that was a bonus!!! Three connects! Life was getting so good. And if they weren't available, we could still put our money up with Flash, ET, and Doc Boog. Flash became a beast. He moved his business so fast it was gone the very next day as he had boys from Garfield, Homewood, and Saint Clair all moving major work. He would sell his, then would sell mine, whatever I had left. It got to a point that everything on the western side of Pennsylvania was being pumped into the communities by one of The Duke Boys, one of the PA Gangstas, or their associates.

It became pointless to ever stay another night at that apartment. I pulled up one day while all the homies were sitting on Speedy John's porch across the street from the apartment. Ms. Lockey's home was the place to be every day. She had beer for sale, and a son that was like that brother that's the same age as you and who understood the way of life. The struggle was always the same way with me from the time we knew who one another was. Every morning, we'd gather on the front or back porch, which the alleyway behind their home led to Burns Heights, constant traffic flowing peacefully every morning hitting all kinds of licks all day long. No matter what Crawford Ave was on fire! That's where the shoulders met. It's where I'd be sure to find a homie that was moving my business for me.

I pulled up in my all-black E320 Lexus and yelled out the window to Speedy John for him to meet me around the back of me and Bowie's apartment real quick. He walked over. I asked him to help me carry my TV and clean whatever I could out of my room. There were just a few things I wasn't taking along with me. I just wanted the clothes packed up and any mail. I left the bed and dressers.

After we loaded up the trunk and backseat of the car, I was out. I handed Pirl the keys and told him to give it to his boy, Bowie City, when he came back from wherever he was. I wished that he was there, though.

From that day forward, it would be a long while before Bowie and I talked again. We'd see each other all the time but didn't speak at all. People that didn't know the whole story still assumed that I got mad at him because he was screwing around with Ke-Ke. That was not the reason at all. That snake had told some chick he laid up with that he was going to kill me.

Cash was going from stacks to pounds rapidly. I kept two thousand dollars on me every day for pocket money. Wrapping ten stacks together at a time now and sending off to be put away. Life was fantastic. I was on my way to the top. I had it all figured out. I'll just come back to the Duke whenever I felt like it. I had workhorses on my squad now from all over the city, from all walks of life. Most of the time, I spent gambling at Swamps, sitting at my grandmother's while the police were calling us menaces to our neighborhood. That may have been partially true, but we were getting involved with the community in a positive way as well. We all pitched in to help get the little kids football equipment and a few of us became coaches. We kept the community going locally. I took what ET had done to me and carried on the tradition. I made sure everyone around me had the opportunity to eat the same way I was. If I liked you and you came to me for some work, I'd ask what you were trying to do, what were your goals, motives, and what consequences were you prepared to deal with if you screwed up some money or got busted by the police. I was enforcing all the rules verbally once, up aside your head after that. My main goal, if I liked you though, was to get you on your feet by allowing you to get on at my wholesale price and start sending your own money at your own risk. My saying was "don't miss the boat!" If you missed the boat, you weren't getting the wholesale price.

Spread Your Wings

I had just gotten back from a seven-day vacation with Monica where we discussed buying a house together before our daughter, Nique, arrived. We had already named her before she was even six months in Monica's tummy. So, we had planned to buy a home on the west side of the city with a $100,000 budget. This would make our love for one another official and we had hopes of marriage within the next two years. We eventually found a home that was a good fit for the family we were starting; the perfect starter home. For less than a hundred grand, we settled on a corner lot home that was equipped with three bedrooms and a beautiful leveled yard. The problem was that it was outdated. The stone brick needed sandblasted all around the house, and then the inside needed a complete upgrade. We planned to install a huge pool out back and a little princess pink room in one of the bedrooms upstairs. We wanted to redo our unfinished basement and add arcade machines. We went and did all this work in such a short amount of time. We closed on our new home just two weeks before the expected due date for Monica. Another very high point in my recent success with the business. I was the youngest and the first of all my homies, even the older ones, to buy a home outside of the hood.

I know a higher being was watching over Monica because to our surprise we completely remodeled our first home together in two short weeks, completing it two days before we welcomed our first daughter together into the world. It was an amazing feeling. I did something good. So young. Finally. I felt my first true accomplishment in life. We also managed to think ahead and placed the home into a very trusted immediate family member's name for safety precautions in case anything had ever happened to us. We purchased and installed an 18 x 33 ft pool for the yard; cut down numerous huge trees and wrapped the pool with a deck. My old head from the Northside, Uncle Mike, knew the perfect contractor that accepted Product for payment for the remodeling work he did. So, the privacy fence we had installed all around, the deck for the pool, the newly remodeled basement, all got done for a super reasonable price once it was all said and done. And it was all done on time by mid-May; just in time for the start of the summer of 1999.

Two weeks before we finalized the purchase of the home, we were sleeping on a Friday night when the house phone rang. Something about that ring I'll never forget because I jumped up and immediately picked up with my heart racing as if I knew it was bad news. And yes, it was heartbreaking news. Tragedy had struck. Rookie's old girlfriend from before he went to prison, Keva, was on the other end of the phone. Keva was also one of Monica's good friends. She said, "Clabo, one of those Braddock boys shot Antwan in the head when he came out of the bar over here." She went on to say what happened and that she didn't think he was alive. I dropped the phone and instantly yelled out, "I told him not to go over there to Braddock after he just shot Hoody in the bar in Duquesne!"

Although we felt that Hoody wasn't going to retaliate, he had young followers behind him that would do something to prove their loyalty with hopes of getting on from him or something. Twan had just told me he was over there the week before and that they were acting funny. Twan had shot Hoody in the bar in Duquesne one night when Hoody was sitting in there with his all blue on as if he was representing himself as a Crip. Twan was a Blood. I conducted business with Hoody. Twan didn't care and he wouldn't listen when I tried to hold him back from shooting Hoody while we were all in the back area of the bar. I had them together after that incident to squash the issue and all was supposedly alright with those two, I thought!!!

Twan ended up passing away while two of his older brothers were in prison, Tee and Rook. Rook was nine years in on a ten-year sentence for homicide already and was soon to be up for parole. There were a couple of stories floating around, but Hoody would not admit that he knew who had done it. It became one of the deals where I was going to keep my friends close and my enemies even closer!

I talked it over with Rook and asked him if he wanted me to take Hoody's head off his shoulders and that it would've been super easy to do because I was still dealing with him regularly. He was one of my good customers. Rook asked me not to do anything to him. He had heard he wasn't the one behind doing that, so we let him have a pass for now. All I had to do was give the word and he would've been dealt with.

So here I am losing my cousin and didn't even get a HEAD in return yet. I now had the money, the power, and the respect to make whatever become a reality. I had Riz, the kid that used to play on my baseball team, now as a customer. He had moved to another part of town and ran that area with my business. I had my old head, Uncle Mike, running the Northside. I could give him five hundred bricks at a time. Put it this way, he always owed me thirty thousand dollars because I always gave him the same amount on consignment that he had bought off me. And he had whole Eagles if I wanted any at any time, which occasionally I would get a couple and resale them for like a quick five-thousand-dollar profit just with it going from his hand to mines and my hand to a profit within an hour or two. Limited work was always the best.

Life Is Good

It was such a beautiful day. My three kids were with me, both of my grandmother's Evelyn and Nelena, Monica's mother and grandmother, and my mother. I had to snap a few pictures from the Canon we had set up on the tripod in the living room. We arranged for this generational picture as I had dreamed for this day to happen. I was just as grateful and happy as I could be. I was now old enough to drink a little vodka with my grandmother Evelyn. And yes, I ran downstairs and pulled a gallon of gin off the shelf and made my way back up to the dining room to pour some gin over some fresh ice to satisfy my Gram's urge to have a drink. Everyone who knew my Gram knew that if she didn't have her drink, she just might simply ignore you or act a little bourgeois. When she had it, she was the nicest lady in the whole world. I would've never thought that would've been the last time she would step foot in my home. Maybe I should've known that as we all knew she didn't like to even come out the house much. So, it was quite a shock that she so willingly got all dressed up to come and sit with me and my new family. Although she was crazy about me! I was her favorite, remember! I was still blind to a lot of things, although I felt as though I was finally free from the confinement and everyday lifestyle of the hustle. But traveling back and forth to Duquesne so often, I was far from free.

I was creating more problems with the more money I was making. I went and bought a brand-new special edition Chevy Tahoe "Cabelo's Edition." The Cabelo's Edition was a green exterior with the tan leather interior which had the Cabelo's name stitched into the headrests of the seats. Not only did I have a new truck, but I also had to put a five thousand dollars speaker system in it with the new 20-inch rims that the rappers were now thumping about and flashing across the television screens. That still wasn't loud enough, so I went and put TVs throughout the inside, too. Now I was doing it big! Soon after, all my homies bought trucks and then brand-new cars after the trucks.

When the Duke boys went out, we had just as much, if not more, attention on us as Jerome Bettis, Hines Ward, Joey Porter and the rest of the Steelers players that were partying in the same night clubs. They were jumping out of brand-new Mercedes and so was Flash as that was his choice of car, the big body Benz. We were pulling up together three or four deep, jumping out valet at Donzies, Chauncey's, and Whiskey Dicks night clubs on Sundays after the games, Wednesdays, and Thursdays. Every night was lit if we were out!

I'll never forget when we were up Greensburg one day at this biracial young lady's house. She was very pretty, had a short haircut, and wicked smile to compliment it. CY had just met her at Chauncey's that past Thursday night, and it was just Friday evening and we were riding up to visit this girl. He sure wasn't wasting any time trying to get to know this girl better. On the ride up, we smoked a cigar and laughed and talked about how she said she was dating a ballplayer, but he wasn't the person he was portrayed to be behind closed doors. We sat and talked as she hosted very well with shrimp cocktails and Heinekens, one of our preferred drinks. We were there about two hours before we heard a knock at the door. We weren't carrying pistols, so I was like, "Yo, what's up? Who's that knocking like that on the door?" She seemed nervous and her face turned beet red and she said, "It's Rome!" I said "Rome?" and looked at CY and burst out laughing. She opened the door and let him in. He looked at us and we looked at him and just nodded our heads. He asked her to step outside and they must've talked all of two minutes before she came back in and said he was very upset and hurt and that he knew who we were. When we finally left, I messed with CY the whole drive home, laughing and stroking his ego about taking Rome's chick!

We had taken over the city of Pittsburgh with our street business. Violent crime was at an all-time low as we allowed every hood in the city to eat, young, older, everyone ate. Robberies, homicides, and thefts were all down. And the city was on fire. When you got out of jail, all you had to do was make an OG call and we answered!

Pray for The Homie

Crump happened to call CY's phone one day while we were all at Swamps gambling, sitting around, smoking and drinking. Crump had graduated from Duquesne University School of Law. He wasn't drafted to the NBA, but he got a contract playing basketball in Spain. He had gone over with his girlfriend. He was on the speakerphone asking what we all were up to and saying how much he missed home. He said the money was decent playing basketball and that his agent was still trying to get him a few tryouts in the NBA. He just needed to work on a few things. Rooskie started telling Crump about all of us buying new cars and when he mentioned business was paying off and CY had just bought a new Cadillac, Crump says "Oh snap… I'm on the next thing smoking. I'm coming home. Forget this basketball stuff!" We all laughed it off and eventually hung the phone up. But to our surprise, he called back a few days later and said he was about to board a flight home. I remember us asking where his girlfriend was, and he replied that he left her in Spain. Her flight wasn't until a couple of days later. They only had one seat left and he was on the first thing smoking! I was like, wow! He is wild for that one there! He was leaving it all to come back to the hood and deal drugs!

He had set himself up for greatness being finally free from the depressed city of Pittsburgh. But somehow, he was being sucked in by temptation and the unknown. When he had a degree and basketball future already secured. He had made the right choices years ago and stayed on the right path. He had sold a little bit of weed to maintain and often hung out with us at the nightclubs and gambling spots. But still, most of the time he had Mike James along with him. But this was a big dangerous move. The wrong move. We all agreed that he was making the wrong move and expressed that to him at one time or another. We preferred that he continued playing ball so we could travel and see him and maybe find a way to invest the money that we were accumulating very fast. He was about to enter a whole different lifestyle.

Although they labeled the drug world "the game" it certainly was not one. It was not a game, at all! In basketball, you win or lose, shake hands and get right back to business. In the streets, you win too much and people hate you, people plot on you, people will kill you to take what you have if you're not careful. If you lose, that could result in you losing your life. Or a loss could mean you are going away FOR YEARS. So many different scenarios and at some point, you were following someone else's lead. Being the captain of this team came with a lot of responsibility and he soon found out just a few months into his new business venture.

He decided he had found the perfect mule to transport packages from state to state. He had been successful a couple of times having this young white girl from a town over in McKeesport make the runs. He would sleep with her occasionally as she was with several other men, including one that was plotting on stealing one of the packages. All the homies typically would make the call and pass it along that the boat was pulling out the next day, so if you wanted to get in you could. Crump was kind of desperate, hungry to climb to the top, so he was going more than anyone else. Once he got the connects numbers, he was off to the races often. Just so happened that he had orchestrated a close to five thousand bundle pick up which amounted to roughly a cool three hundred and fifty thousand dollars. When that package got back it would have yielded over a million dollars in return.

Crump had the old heads in on it. ET, Flash, Doc Boog, and a few others. Not respecting and following protocol correctly and having trust in a female that don't even trust or care about herself, resulted in him not following her on the way back with the package and allowed her to simply drive the package straight to Nitty and put it in his hand without him having to physically rob anyone with a gun. The biggest and easiest heist ever pulled off that I heard about up to that point in my life.

Once he said that she wasn't answering the phone, everyone strapped up and went to find her. She wasn't anywhere to be found but her sister was, and she was placed in one of the vehicles under tight wraps and restraints. She eventually told what she knew and where she had known her sister and Nitty to frequent and lay low at. They were nowhere to be found.

Crump had come back and messed up big time. There was some talk about duct-taping him up and throwing him in the river. Confirmation word soon got out that it was exactly true that Nitty had got out on the Duke Boys. War soon followed. But without missing a beat, packages continued to roll in as if that didn't faze the homies who all took that loss.

Bowie City never invested with anyone. He was friends with Nitty. That was his connect way before the incident took place! I wondered if he was in on that being that they were our only competition. We'd soon find out because in every hood we had eyes and ears waiting to see who would be trying to move anything with that stamp name on it. The first time anyone's name was mentioned that was said to have that name, they were immediately dealt with, which caused an all-out war in a few different neighborhoods. This was the result of someone trying to be and do something that they weren't called to do in their life. The trickledown effect wasn't good at all.

West West Ya'll

CY and I were hanging almost every day now. We were rolling big time; my cousin Reub was also. Life was great. For my daughter's first birthday party, we threw a huge house party in the backyard replete with a full-fledged DJ and the Teletubbies in full costume for the kids. My daughter loved the Teletubbies on TV but was scared when she saw them in person. She was just turning one year old. She didn't have a clue how she was being spoiled or what was even taking place. She'd have plenty of pictures to look at when she was old enough to understand, though.

Money was rolling in and I still didn't have a plan. I liked the idea of buying another house though, as I had become familiar with the neighborhood now where we lived. Being the social butterfly Monica was she arranged with the owner of the local beer distributor to look at a rental property he was selling in the nearby McKees Rocks area. I went along and looked at it with Monica and agreed to buy it for $15,000, which was under the asking price of $20,000. Being that we were offering to pay cash for it, he agreed. He had more properties that he said he would eventually be willing to sell.

Mr. D. was an old Italian guy that gave me some knowledge on how to conduct real estate business. I was all ears as I listened to every word he spoke while a cigar dangled from his lips. I decided to put this house in my name so that I could start establishing myself within the real estate world as he had told me to do. Maybe I could make real estate my way out to someday be legit. I was sure going to try.

Tee had just come home and received an OG call from his little cousin. He couldn't believe how much money I had, the house that I had bought on his side of town, nor that I was with Monica someone that he knew very well. I gave Tee $10,000 and told him to pay me back when he flipped it a few times. He did exactly that and brought plenty of business from the west side back along with him. It was nothing but love all over.

I was sitting on the porch with my daughter swinging in the electric swing that always kept her nice and calm when I noticed a grey Lexus hit the corner with a Keith Sweat song playing. As the car pulled up closer, I noticed a dark-skinned man with sunglasses on smiling from ear to ear. It was Tee. This guy here done went and purchased an LS430 and was looking like he could barely see over the steering wheel. The shortest guy went and bought the biggest car. It wasn't even a month from the time he got out of jail that he had already got himself a new car, a luxury car. I let him know that I thought that was a bad move. I felt as though he should've purchased a home first then got himself a little runner to make moves in. My goodness! He looked nice and happy that day, though. We sat and talked for a while about the latest happenings before his phone rang. Rodney was on the other line saying he had just got back out of jail and was trying to get on. He put me on the phone. We talked and I told him I'd see him next time I was over the Duke.

Rodney always had an attitude with somebody. Not many people liked to deal with him because they were afraid of him not paying or just having the bully mentality. He knew he had none of that fear with me, though. He knew I would handle my business without a second thought. If you showed any fear to someone like that, he would always feed off that and would continue to try to bully you. He liked to fight when we were younger and was known for being a troublemaker. I think he got the most paddles in school by Mr. Perrin, our principal! Up until the point where he would just refuse and then he would get suspended.

I made my point very clear when I finally met him. I gave him a thousand dollars and ten bricks and told him to hook up with Reub and he would let him eat with him. That went on all for about three weeks until

Reub went on the run for a homicide charge they were accusing him of.

Reub was the reason all his little boys under him following his lead made any money to survive. He was the reason things remained peaceful somewhat while he was around. He went on the run and ran straight up to Philly and Jersey where our connects were. He tried to run his operation on his own from there, but his little dirtball boys were starting to mess up his money, so he asked if I would just handle his money and flip it and send him a few thousand up with every move I made. That wasn't a problem unless the connect was coming to Pittsburgh.

Rodney wanted in, but Reub wanted him out as he had messed up some money also. I decided we would help my other cousin out and let him move all of Reub's work, which worked out just fine. Everything was still all under control. Reub wanted to sell the duplex he had just purchased before the homicide accusations being made, so I bought it. He hadn't had time to fix the duplex that was just a block from the police station in the hood. My first piece of property where I grew up. Another accomplishment to be grateful for!

No Slippin' Baby

"*I see your sneakers getting dingy. I see your jealousy and your envy! You ain't got no paper though*!" was what I heard when I opened the door to the studio

Crump had put together next to the barbershop where the apartment, I had previously subleased from my sister was. "*You ain't got no paper though*!" Crump was laughing saying come on everybody get in the booth and scream the hook.

Yes, we had just started a record label, Iced Out Records. Well ET, Doc Boog, Flash, and Crump did. Tee, CY and I started an LLC called No Slippin' Records. We joined together and produced the War Team Album soon after. That was our new focus. We would produce music, hire the top talent, record hits, and promote them by bringing nationally renowned famous artists to local venues and have our artists open up the shows. That first single he made had everyone that was jealous extremely jealous now! Nobody wanted to be that one with the dingy sneakers on either. Shoe sales skyrocketed. Were we ready for the attention that the music was going to bring? I guess that answer depended on who you asked.

According to JuJu, we were on to something, but it would require him to get involved and sign on with No Slippin' as the featured artist. We agreed to sign him on being that he was solid and had a particular fan base in the city. He went by the name Nikki Scarfa and had a whole album already stored in his head. "Dangerous Money's What I Live For" was one of my favorites. Maybe because it was true; we were living to make the dangerous money.

We took our studio time seriously and decided to only record at Soundscape Studios with a top-notch engineer and state of the art equipment. We were off doing our music at a different studio, but we all went to New York to shoot for the "You Ain't Got No Paper" video. We rented two 15 passenger vans and drove to Harlem for the shoot.

After a long day of filming, we were in and out of the hotel and one another's rooms when I saw Shon laughing and waving me on but saying be quiet. He had the door to Crump's room cracked open. He told me to look and when I did, I saw Crump on the floor on top of somebody humping up and down forcefully. As I shut the door back, Shon says, "Dog, I was outside and this homeless lady…" I burst out laughing with a loud, "Ewwwww that is nasty!"

I waited by the door and when she came out of the hotel room, I asked her name. She said "Nadine." I asked her, "Where do you live?" She explained that she lived under the bridge. Her hair was really dirty, and she smelled like she hadn't bathed in weeks. I reached into my pocket and counted out four twenty-dollar bills and handed them to her and said, "Go clean yourself up!"

Crump was so mad at me because I went around and told all the homies that one of Iced Out Records' executives and main artist just laid pipe to a homeless lady that lives under the bridge. Oh my goodness! From that day on I was convinced that he was the nastiest person I had ever known in my life. Here he was shooting a major video by day and sleeping with a random homeless woman at night. I never could quite understand that. Other than that, the experience of traveling out to NY for the video shoot was fun and worthwhile.

Back at home in Pittsburgh, I was introduced to the comedian Michael Blackson through a mutual promoter, Muhammad. In the mix of that introduction, I met Tim. Tim was Michael's manager and brother-in-law. Tim was from New York and had several resources and ideas I thought were valuable to our ultimate goal - climbing the charts as fast as possible. This venture was the first disagreement that Monica and I had. She said it was a waste because all I wanted to do was run around and hook up with different groupies in different cities while she stayed at home with my children. She didn't like that I would be out of town or at the studio more than I was home. I was either at the studio, out of town, or running around conducting business. Sundays were always the day I'd relax and sit around and flick the channels all day.

On Who's Grave

Here we were in the spring of 2000 on our way to Cancun for spring break. It was just all the homies, all twelve of us, flying first class and ready to have a good time. The flight was great. We laughed about Crump once again because he decided to fly in a day before us to Cancun to "get a jump on things." He had certainly done just that. He was sending us messages saying he had everything lined up for us at the hotel already and had reserved twelve scooters for us and had twelve presents for us to pick up once we got our scooters and were all changed and showered and ready for the day. We all laughed and were excited to see just what presents he had for us. Once we landed and had retrieved our luggage, Crump was pulling up on a scooter with his long lanky 6'6 frame bunched up on what looked like a scooter for 10-year old's. But what we all took notice of was the eye candy he had on the back of it. She looked like the centerfold I had just seen in the KING magazine while on the flight. She had on a bikini and cover with pretty white teeth glistening in the Mexican sun. We all looked, laughed, and exchanged our pleasantries before jumping in the taxis and following his lead with the undersized and outdated helmet he had on. Not even five minutes down the road, we turned up into the driveway to our hotel. We paid the taxi drivers and they moved right along. Once we checked in and got quick showers, we all met back up in the lobby, grabbed a drink, and headed across the street to pay for the scooters he had reserved.

The Latino workers at the spot gave us strict orders to be careful from the police by making sure you wear your helmet. Well, that didn't sit well with a few of us. But as the adage goes, "a hard head makes a soft behind!" As soon as we pulled out onto the street following Crump to the surprise, he said he had for us, the police yanked us over within one block from where we started from just a second ago.

Three officers jumped out of an '81 K car, walked up to us and said, "Usted, usted, and usted! Off de bicicleta ahora!" They were pointing and saying "You, you, and you! Off the bikes, now!" They were pointing at me, ET, and Speedy John Pirl. "The law says you go to jail in Mexico, my friend, for no wear helmet, my friend. Only way no jail is $100, now!" These Mexican police officers were straight jacking us off the top not even an hour into the trip. We talked them down to $50 each and were back on our way.

The strip was lit. It was a beautiful day; the sun was nice and bright, and people were out everywhere. We are in the thick of it enjoying our lives and cruising down Blvd Kukulkan in Cancun. We rode about 12 kilometers down the road and dipped off up in front of another hotel. Crump's lady friend excused herself from the back of his bike and disappeared into the hotel. Two minutes later she reappears with a group of gorgeous girls following behind her. They looked us up and down while we did the same to them mentally deciding who wanted to ride with who. Moments later we were off. Every one of them had jumped on the back of someone's bike and not one girl was left standing when we pulled off. We had thirteen gorgeous young ladies from California on our bikes without any conversation or questions asked. There was no hassle, no meet and greet, no nothing. Just like whatever, what's up! If this is how this is going to be then we are in for a very long trip.

Crump had dinner reserved for a party of thirty! He led us to this nice steak and seafood restaurant and things got a little more intimate and interesting. Everybody had their helmets off and we could finally see each other clearly and check out each other's features and mannerisms up close and personal. Every lady was at least a high eight or better. Crump came through for the homies! Finally!

The only problem was we all had women at home that loved us, missed us and wanted us to remain faithful on this all men's spring break vacation. None of us were married, but each of us might as well had been. Or maybe not because we were all still snakes in the grass at the time.

We ate, had a few drinks, and took the ladies back to their hotel. Well maybe a few of us took the ladies back. Rooskie and Lump stayed right there at the bar in the restaurant. It was still early in the day and there was plenty of time to do whatever. I had a boatload of fun and met some decent people along the journey. We partied all night and day literally like non-stop. I was so happy to be back home though kissing and cuddling with Monica and my baby girl. I was anxious to get back in the studio along with making my rounds to pick up cash from anyone ready and waiting on my return.

Just like that, I was right back in the mix of it all making moves back to back as it was always extremely busy after being gone for a while whether it was just a weekend getaway or an extended vacation. I made my way to my mother's house that she purchased with her new husband. She was doing so well. She had truly turned her life around and she was finally free from the wicked drugs she had quit cold turkey. Free from the days when she would probably do a lot of strange things to chase the high. 'Hallelujah! God delivered my mother, totally. She is finally free!' I screamed as I walked to my brand-new jaguar. I had just bought it a few weeks before I left for vacation. I knew she had been clean for years but seeing her smiling, happy at peace, relaxing this day just sent a tingle up my spine a feeling of joy through my soul.

I headed over to the studio to meet with Nikki Scarfa and his little brothers, Maine, Pa, and Fifty Gs, to listen to some of the songs they had in their head. After hearing them, I immediately wanted them to sign.

They were commercial. I could visualize them on stage in front of a huge audience with all the songs they were freestyling to me. I went in my pocket and gave them a stack a piece and told them, "It's on. We gon' blow up!"

I made a call to Big Dee and told him I had some heat coming his way, and that Black Caesar needed to get ready. I had some young boys from Birmingham, Alabama that had an album in their head already, but they needed top-notch tracks to ride on. I dropped them off with Big Dee and Black Caesar and continued making moves. Later that night, they called me and asked me to come back through. I walked in the spot and heard, "*Eww e eww ahh ahh ting tang wally wally bing bang,*" repeating over and over with a beat that had me stopped in my tracks just bobbing my head like *Wow! That's It!* I knew it. Then they were like, "Hold up. Play the next one, Ceez!" He put on something similar to The Benson's theme song for their TV show and Maine looked at me and said, "*I'mma keep on keeping on no matter what what. I'mma keep on keeping on.*" They switched tracks up and "*Say it. Uh huh, uhhhuh, uh uhu, say it!*"

These boys had hit after hit. God put it right in my hands now. Either I would wake up, slow down, and focus on the blessing that was right before my face or I'd continue to play in the fire. I wanted to get with some of the best producers. So through another mutual friend,

I managed to get with Sam Sneed who was down in Atlanta. He had worked with Tupac and Dr. Dre and was a Pittsburgh native. We managed to put together the album titled "Nothin' You Can Do About It" and decided we would promote it the best we could.

I had Tim in New York connecting on his end. He put something together and got us on DJ Kool Kid's mixtape and had us perform at a small venue in NYC where AR's and music folks were known to frequent for a cocktail after work. After further talks with Tim and the feedback he got along with Big Dee's knowledge, they wanted us to go back to Birmingham and create a local base to stir up a buzz in their hometown, as well as in Pittsburgh. That was all they had to tell me. I was on it!

I got with Mohammed and let him know that we wanted to start promoting shows and we would intend to open up for the artist we brought in to perform. The first artist we had come in was Ludacris with his hot new single "What's Your Fantasy." We sold the place out. Iced Out and No Slippin' was on the map locally. We passed out snippets and t-shirts. It was a good turnout. I remember that day well.

Before the show, we had reserved the top floor of the hotel that was connected to the event. We had a pre-party with strippers, etc. I'll never forget Rick Scott becoming famous in the hood for being called "Sprinkle

Me." Rick always wanted to curse females out and never seemed to get along with any girls. On this particular night, he managed to pay one of the strippers to entertain him personally in the bathroom. The radio in the room stopped and we heard the girl say, "Wait, wait, get up. I gotta pee," and in reply, Rick said, "So what. Just pee! I don't care. Sprinkle Me!" Everyone who heard it started laughing so hard and his new nickname became "Sprinkle Me."

Change the Game

It's a new day and the same old folks were posted up on the same old block. I pulled up and got out to open the side door to the conversion van that I crept around the hood in when I wanted to be low key to stay one step ahead of the local police. I grabbed a full unopened box and handed it to VO and gave him fifty dollars and asked him to pass out all those flyers throughout the hood. I wanted him to put them on utility poles, cars, and local bars. The flyer had just come in for our next show which was featuring Avant. This was something to get all the ladies out for a night out with The Duke Boys. We were heading out the following week for a major marketing event in Miami for the music industry. Every week we were making moves. Nikki Scarfa hung out with Wesley Snipes that weekend. Scarfa would dress up in his suits and derby hats with a fresh pair of gators on his feet. He would talk that straight gangsterism nonstop. I couldn't believe those two were on the dance floor smoking cigars together. Nothing surprised me much nowadays. While we were in Miami, we ran across Ludacris again with his DTP crew and this time we had a full-length cd to give him. He respectfully accepted it and he must have liked it because the "Ting Tang Wally Wally Bing Bang" ended up on a song on his next album. From Miami, we drove to Alabama to see what kind of buzz we could create. Maine took us straight to the hood and being that it was later in the evening when we arrived, we hit up the local bars. We blended right in and got the party started. We passed out snippets, flyers, and t-shirts and bought drinks for the entire bar. At the same time, we worked our way over to the DJ. After about three songs, we were hearing No Slippin's name announced and the music beating through the speakers. "I was all about handling my biz, cabbage, and bread." And not just me, it was like I adopted my artists. I took care of every single one of them daily- apartments, allowances, advances; blessings that you can't measure. By no means did I allow any of the personal business I was conducting to be put upon any of my artists. I kept them far away from it as best as I could.

Studio time and the traveling, doing shows, entertaining the crowds large and small, the long car rides from state to state; all of this was peaceful to me. It was my way to escape the constant phone calls and running around risking my life from day-to-day. I was kind-hearted when it came to helping and providing for others. I would climb in the back of our conversion van, lay the bed down, turn a movie on and zone out. No phone. No pager. No Monica bickering in my ear. Just a peace of mind. Finally free from all my problems when I hit the road!

Alabama was where we stayed three nights then got up early in the a.m. and jumped on I-65 and headed back to PA. Twelve hours later, we were pulling up at my doorstep. Once again, I was so happy to be home. The Avant show was quickly approaching, and it ended up being another success.

A few weeks later, we did Absolut and Little Mo at the same venue on the South Side of Pittsburgh and that sold out. Everything we touched seemed to turn to gold. Things were rolling right along. Rook got released and I broke him off the same way as I did Tee. My brother got out a few weeks after also. He was a little different. He didn't like or want anyone looking out too much. He'd rather grind himself. Besides, he didn't like handling the business that we were all into. He enjoyed soaring with the Eagles.

Chapter Fourteen

Laugh Now, Cry Later

The table was surrounded by young boys, OGs, and old-timers. Even Old Man Joe from the Hill District was in attendance at Swamps spot. Cigars were flowing freely. Heineken and Hennessy also. People were in and out. I threw a stack down and stopped the bank just at the right time. Three-three-one popped up on the dice and Swamp just looked with his old looking puppy face. I scraped the money up, sorted the bills out, counted out $860.00 total profit and made my bank $500.00. Win or lose, I was done after my roll. The kids had football practice up Polish hill and I was going to check them out. ET jumped in his Range Rover and we all headed up there. Earlier that day, ET and I were talking, and he had mentioned that the package that just came through would put him over the million-dollar mark once it was sold. He told me he had invested one hundred and twenty thousand dollars. I hadn't even hit five hundred thousand yet and he was at a million in the millennium ending the summer of 2000 on a very high note. A major milestone coming from the projects. Nearly every hustler's dream was to hit seven figures. For some reason, we talked like never before. He just opened up to me this day. He told me that he felt some of the homies wouldn't put work in for him, that he had seen something different in some people after he had got shot on the parkway coming from Donzie's club that night. I couldn't believe I was hearing this. I remembered us all hanging together every single day. Maybe he knew something that I didn't know! That night when someone pulled up alongside his bubble eyed GS 430 Lexus and sprayed the car up had us all puzzled and had everyone, we knew from every hood listening and keeping their ears to the streets to try and find out who had attempted to assassinate our number one big homie. At this point, justice was going to be sold from our point of view to the highest bidder! ET went on to say that he was about to be done hustling once that package was sold. He always told me that after he got shot, he saw it in some of the homies eyes that they didn't want to ride he went on to say he was ready to die and that he knew he wouldn't live long with the seizures he suffered with from time to time. He told me to keep my eyes on them too because they were jealous of the way I was making things happen. I listened closely to every word he was speaking. Just like I did when I asked him over and over to get on my song for my album and at least get in the booth and say something. And he did say something per my request. He got in the booth and said, "In these streets, it ain't what you know, it's who you know" as the intro to my song "In These Streets." He then went on to tell me that my little cousin Marv had come downstairs in the middle of the night while

ET was being intimate with Marv's mother. He said Marv just looked then went back upstairs stomping on the steps loud and hard on his way up. He also said that he like Little Marv and had just fronted him two ounces of business the day before that. He said he also enjoyed the mothers' company even though she and his live-in girlfriend were good friends. We laughed and talked a little more before I jumped in my Tahoe and hit the back roads out of town and into the city. I told everyone I'd see them tomorrow around the same time for football.

Well, the next day rolled around and just like the day before we started at the gambling spot. Something seemed a little eerie on this sunny day of September. September 6th, to be exact. The sun would shine and then it would just pour down raining in spurts; there was even thunder and lightning at times. Then the sun would pop back out from behind a dark cloud and dry up all the rain. I remember standing inside Swamps and just gazing out the window wondering if football would go on or not. Surprisingly, it did go on and today ET had decided to leave his Range Rover parked near Swamps and jumped in the truck with me to ride up to Polish Hill. No sooner than we got there, the kids started arriving, and a police car pulled up. The cop exited his car and started walking over to us all. It was Van Smitty, a black cop who we all knew. He was the only cop that didn't attempt to harass us daily. He walked up and started talking just as my phone rang. I answered my phone, Monica was on the other end saying that she wanted me to come home and spend some time with her. I told her that I would be home in about an hour or so and to hold on for a minute while I listened to what this cop was saying to the homies. He said practice had to be suspended immediately because there wasn't any insurance placed on the field. I thought it was bullcrap that the police were even checking up on that kind of stuff. Was this something to try and hold us back from allowing the children to chase their dreams? Control was what they wanted! They didn't care about the kids and community or else they would have handled this situation differently. They could have at least given us a heads up so we could have prepared ourselves ahead of time.

We broke the bad news to the kids, the parents, and anyone else who was listening. I let the homies know that as soon as the cop left that I was leaving. I had a large sum of money in my truck that I was not willing to jeopardize, and have it taken by the police. I asked ET what he was going to do. I told him that I wanted to hit the back way from Polish Hill to go home, but I would ride him back down if he wanted me to. He told me that he was alright, that CY was there, and that he would just ride with him. I gave him some brotherly love and said I was out.

I jumped in my truck and headed towards the West Side. I got home, showered, and went out to eat with my family. As soon as we got back in about 8 pm my phone rang. I didn't answer the first time because I was holding my daughter talking baby talk. The phone rang again. It was CY calling right back. I picked it up thinking something must be wrong. And it was. He sounded startled and was screaming "E got shot! The young boys shot E! We need you to come now, Dog, we gotta get these boys!"

I instantly started shaking. My palms got sweaty as I was pacing around trying to gather my thoughts. I grabbed my pistol and the keys to my van and headed out. I called CY back, but he didn't answer. So I moved on to the next homie and Flash answered. He said they rushed E to the closest hospital and that it doesn't look good; he isn't responsive. I asked what happened, but he wouldn't tell me. He said just get over here.

By the time I made it to McKeesport Hospital, everyone was standing and sitting outside the emergency room entrance very quiet. It didn't look good. I walked up, walked past everyone outside, and entered the ER. I was met by Sweet T. She was crying and I hugged her. "They took my baby. Clabo, he's gone. They took my baby!"

How did this happen? Where did this happen? And why did it happen? This man would give you the shirt off his back if you asked for it. And not just my friend, brother, or homie. This was the whole hood's big homie. He tattooed my heart early in my adolescent years.

ET made the impossible possible early in the hood. No way in the world was this happening. I had to keep my composure and stay strong, just as he had been to me a couple of days before this. I embraced his mother and said I was sorry and promised her that it would be okay. What did I mean by that? How could it be okay? The only way it was going to be okay in my eyes was to find out who did it! So I had to ask her that very question, "Do you know who did it?" "Yep, we do. It was Little Marv and Pee Wee," she responded. "They said ET went into Swamps and was gambling, Clabo. Someone rang the doorbell. Swamp opened the door because he knew who it was. Then Pee-Wee and Marv pulled out guns and attempted to rob my baby. They said E told them he wasn't giving them anything and that they had to shoot him. They ran off and some of the boys are over there now looking for them!" I looked at her with disgust. E just gave him two ounces so he could make some money! So many abnormal thoughts were now going through my head. What had just taken place? I felt an instant emptiness in my heart. These fools took my protégé. I felt stuck between a rock and a hard place. What do I do? Do I just let the other homies do what they feel needs to be done?

It didn't take long to find out they were arrested just as fast as they had done it. That was the best thing that they could have done at that time was to turn themselves in because the heat was on them from every angle. I could never understand why my big homie didn't just give them the money and have them dealt with the following day! I believe they didn't want his money. I believe someone sent them on a wild goose chase solely because of jealousy and envy. Then the conversation that E and I just had days prior replayed in my mind. E was tired and most of all he was prepared. He expressed his readiness. God called him home on September 6th, 2000.

Everything changed. The hood was on fire, especially after one of their little friends was gunned down soon after. Duquesne turned into a mini Chicago or Iraq. Gunshots became a normal sound. Fortunately, I had moved out of there. Out of sight, out of mind. As much as I like to gamble and frequent Swamps, I never stepped foot in that place again. Rodney had started influencing those little kids that weren't but 14 and 15 years old, so I completely cut him off. And he couldn't go through my cousin Reub to get on either.

Do you see the connection? When everybody eats in the hood the violent crime goes down. It's a vicious cycle. I started having nights that I couldn't sleep. I missed my big homie. Things weren't the same without him. I'd be up in the middle of the night writing music in remembrance of ET. "I'mma Ride 4 E" became a hood hit. I collaborated with some heavy hitters on a few tracks. I was inspired to release my album "Deep Inside the Game" which featured artists from all over Pittsburgh.

I connected with Monica's cousin DJ Spoon on the west side and Big Willie and his peoples. My workers had workers nowadays. I wasn't touching hardly anything. I let Rook take over everything. He was always on point, business-minded, and street smart just as I was. So while I was traveling and focusing on the music, he was back in the city making sure everything ran smooth and blowing up at the same time. I could trust him to do whatever and be certain that it would run smooth. He kept the peace. He saved Rodney from harm this particular time. I had had words with Rodney one day at my cousin Moe Joe's house. I told him, "I don't just like bodies. I like the head," which meant I'm coming for the top person. When I come, I'm not just going to do something to a street soldier. I'm coming for the one who's brainwashing the street soldiers.

Welcome to Atlanta

Several months had passed since E was killed. At the beginning of the year, all of us had decided to go to the Superbowl in Atlanta. While there, we encountered an ice storm over the weekend. Flash was driving his brand-new Cadillac Escalade when he lost control on the ice and smacked a pole head-on. The OnStar came on over the speaker and said, "Mr. Carter, are you alright? Help is on the way!" Mr. Carter was the person's name to whom the vehicle was registered as we never put vehicles in our names. That was my introduction to OnStar! We called ourselves going to a party Disturbing the Peace was having, but we never made it. We ended up being smacked in the face by airbags. It wasn't quite the weather described by my friend who lived in Atlanta. It was cold just like back home.

While in Cancun, I had met a young lady that was from Atlanta. So when we visited Atlanta for the first time, she welcomed us to her home. When we arrived at her place, the homies were somewhat blown away at the size of her home. She had a huge home; seven bedrooms and five full bathrooms. She showed us what southern hospitality was all about. She had dinner made for us and she offered to let all the homies stay there. She called her girlfriends up and we had a nice get together. She was all business and had a lot of positive things going for herself. No kids, two degrees, a beautiful home, and a personality to match. She eventually also wanted more than I could give. Seeing her home and talking with her, my homies started saying that they wanted to move to Atlanta. So she goes on to tell me that she can make that happen. Her mother was a realtor and could get them any house they wanted as long as they could put ten percent up for the down payment. With all that said, I arranged for her mother to meet us that Sunday early in thc morning to show us some homes. She showed us the homes as well as different model homes. Then showed us empty lots where the home would be built. Doc Boog, and Flash were all in. They wanted to move!

Doc Boog ended up being the first one who moved down to Atlanta! He used my friend's mother to find a home and finalized the deal.

Flash also moved his family to Atlanta just minutes away from Doc Boog. I wasn't moving anywhere. I had a lovely home with the perfect yard and a legit business to run while I kept it afloat with my illegal business. But them moving there just gave me another reason to visit there more often. And that's exactly what I did.

I met a very good guy named L while I was visiting one weekend. The same weekend me, Flash, and one of his daughters were on an AirTran flight from Pittsburgh to Atlanta one day when we experienced a bad flight. We were sitting near the rear of the plane as it had just taken off and was ascending into the clouds. Suddenly hot air started blowing out of the overhead A/C vent followed by *Ding. Ding. Ding* and emergency lights. Then total silence. The plane started to get so hot that sweat was pouring from my underarms and forehead. Maybe it was the total silence, or the look Flash gave me or even the response and look on the flight attendants' faces. You could hear a pin drop. That's how quiet the plane was. Then the pilot came over the intercom and said, "We have an emergency, ladies, and gentlemen. We will be turning around and going back to Pittsburgh."

Yes, we can all tell there is an emergency Mr. Pilot. These are not the words I wanted to hear! I looked at Flash and said "It's over Ace. We about to blow up!" He didn't say a word. He just hugged his little girl tightly.

God had a different plan because we made it back with the 737 still in one piece. I let out a sigh of relief and thanked God. I wasn't trusting the Lord with all my heart, though. I didn't understand that with Christ all things would be made possible. I had more praise for the influencers on the block sitting at what looked like the top. I was introduced to the good news and knew right from wrong. But I was focused on being self-centered, ego-driven, and blind to reality. Blind to the fact that God had given me chance after chance, life, a breath of fresh air just when I doubted with little faith. I was promoting "Only God Can Judge Me" in the streets and using it as an excuse, a crutch when someone didn't agree with the way I had done something. I was liable to tell you to mind your business, screw you and end with "Only God Can Judge Me!"

In the streets on the rise to the top, some folks don't allow anyone or anything to slow them down or get in their way. That flight that day slowed me down and put things into perspective. Had I prepared my family and kids in case I had died? Not quite. Actually, not at all! I hadn't taught my children much if anything at all up until this point. And no matter how much money I left behind that still wouldn't amount to a child being without their father.

I became determined and motivated but remained naïve. I was determined to challenge myself to break the vicious chains and cycle of not knowing our fathers and get things in order so that my children could have a better opportunity than I had. So they wouldn't be susceptible to hearing gunshots at night or seeing another person getting their head blown off. I wanted them to be able to rest at night with peace and quiet. I couldn't bear the thought of them being subjected to poverty nor bars lined up on each corner.

One thing for sure was those were just thoughts, visions, and dreams. I'd have a lot of work to do to get there.

We hopped on Delta after they tried to get us to board the same plane 50 minutes later. We landed in Atlanta a couple of hours later and it was nothing but love as usual. Big L had the limo waiting as he had always done since meeting him.

I met Big L one night when we were all out during Super Bowl weekend. He was a standup guy, an international OG. Anytime I flew in and didn't drive, he had given me the go-ahead to contact my same driver and have him pick me up from the airport and drive me around the whole time I was in town. Real talk, all he wanted me to do was tip the driver. I'd pull up at Doc's or Flash's and have the limo sitting idle while I checked in with my big homies. I felt like a superstar; not only felt it, it was a reality. I was doing it. I was living the good life.

After a laid-back Thursday evening, I was looking forward to Friday afternoon's meeting with Big L. He wanted to take me past his gumbo restaurants and discuss a few things. We met up in Buckhead and headed to his spot. He kept trying to call his head cook and couldn't get through. He said that concerned him because he always answered. We made it to the restaurant, sat down for lunch, and discussed a few power moves before his phone rang. He stepped away and took the call. When he came back, we continued talking and eating as if the call had never taken place. Then after we finished our intense bossed up conversation, we agreed on the topic that was discussed, shook hands, and smiled, "it's all good Bro." He then said, "Oh yeah. That phone call I just got. That was my head cook's people on the phone. He committed suicide. He shot himself in the head."

Everywhere I turned it seemed that death was around the corner. As the evening set in, we were ready for the nightlife. Riding in the stretched limo, smoking and drinking, the homies thought it would be amusing to ride over Bowie City house to pick him up despite the fact I hadn't seen or heard from him since moving out of the apartment. Yes, they were trying to get us to squash the beef. I had already given him a pass a long time ago before I moved out of the apartment all the way. Doc called him on the phone and asked if he wanted to step out for a few drinks. He must have said yes because Doc directed the driver towards THEIR home. Not knowing that it was my limo or that I was inside the limo or even in town! I'll never forget the look on his face when he got into the limo and saw me sitting there! He was so mad at Doc. Doc says to him, "Let that go. Y'all need to let that go, Bowie." He was probably angrier that they showed me where he was living at! I didn't have any ill intent or motive, though. I was living my best life, enjoying the life of luxury. We shook hands and that was that; nothing more, nothing less. We went on with the night and had a really fun time……. Things were really coming together on a major level.

I stayed in town another two days and had to get back to the 'Burgh. Reub was calling me. He needed a couple of thousand dollars as which was his usual every two weeks. Being on the run is very costly, but as long as he had the money, he was alright. He bounced around from Jersey, Philly, New York, and back to Pittsburgh occasionally. Just as I was about to board my flight, Monica called and said cuz had just got to my house and was asking to come in. She knew the procedure. Nobody, absolutely nobody, was allowed in without talking and confirming it with me first. I confirmed and she let him in and welcomed him to the lower level of the house to relax until I touched down in a couple of hours. I was upset because I didn't want him back in Pittsburgh; he was supposed to stay up there. But after talking to him, I understood that life on the run was lonely, and stressed to the max.

Once I got back, the first thing I did was head straight downstairs to see what was up with him. He was like, "Cuz, check this out," as he went on and pulled out some coin bag business and asked me to put it out there. He said he met a new plug and he didn't like them because they went behind Junior's back and was trying to undercut him and do business. He said they would even be willing to bring it to Pittsburgh and would front it without any money upfront. He then said he wanted me to take the package off them. I was definitely with that! I made a call to my old head on the North Side and he came straight through and grabbed it off us and promising he would get back to me within an hour. He did just that and it was alright. Got a seven on a scale from one to ten, which meant that we'd be able to move it. That was all we needed to hear. It was now time to proceed. "Make the call, Cuz," I told him. He did make the call. They answered and said they would get to working on it immediately. Cuz said he needed a few grand to hold him over and he was going back up the way. I gave him five thousand and sent him on the road with one of our designated drivers that were always one phone call away.

In the meantime, in-between time, I went jewelry shopping. I made a few calls and reserved dinner for four up on Mount Washington overlooking the beautiful city of Pittsburgh. Then I made a call to Monica and asked her to get dressed we were going to dinner. We had a built-in babysitter because her mother lived just around the corner, so it was all good. Everything went just right on this day. I had my homie meet me along with his girlfriend. We arrived at the valet at the same time and were promptly seated for dinner. The scene was perfect. All glass windows with a picture-perfect view. We ordered our dinner and appetizers. When the appetizers arrived, I knew it was the time according to the plan. It was at this moment that I got down on one knee and took Monica's hand, looked her in the eyes, and asked if she would marry me while pulling out and sliding a three-carat marquise cut diamond engagement ring on her finger. She looked puzzled and excited as tears streamed down her cheeks. I told her it was time. I knew in my heart long before this day she was the one I wanted to spend my life with. She agreed that she loved me wholeheartedly and was in it for a lifetime. It was a great day. The entire restaurant gave a round of applause.

Later that night, we talked and anyone who knows her knows that when she focuses on a task she obsesses and goes super hard until the task is complete. As we laid in the bed and talked plans and ideas were being thrown around. I had one or maybe two things that were to take place. One was that fifty thousand dollars was the budget and not a penny more! The second was that I had to make it one more summer which meant 2001 was supposed to be the summer to tighten up as we set the date for the end of the summer of 2002.

Intoxicated for The Power

I was happy when cuz called a couple of days after and said they were on their way to the spot and should be there by midnight. I called CY and told him to be on standby; it was on. As the clock struck midnight, my phone rang simultaneously. Cuz said they were at the spot and gave the room number. We were there in a heartbeat. The only issue was, we didn't have our driver with us. But I was willing to take a chance. It was worth it, I thought. We met them. They barely spoke English, which made things that much better! Head nods and yea, yea, yea was all we said. This was the easiest robbery ever. No gun, no drama!!! They went straight to the car and activated the secret compartment and handed over a pretty hefty sized duffle bag. They did ask us to bring thirty thousand dollars back. We said alright, sit tight, we will be back. We pulled off with 1500 bricks knowing we weren't coming back at all. We had just hit a major lick for over a hundred sixty thousand dollars without anybody getting hurt. What were they going to do? They couldn't tell Junior or any of their peoples because they had gone behind their boss's back and backdoored them. More snakes in the grass. All my life all I been around is snakes. The snake cut his own head off this time!

I didn't waste any time moving it. I gave my old head 500 bricks and grabbed the money he owed me from a prior re-up and went and bought my fiancée a brand-new Lincoln Navigator. Money and Power was what it was all about. I had both along with a couple of straight head bussers just a call away. Cuz on the run, five of my other cousins on the squad getting money with me. Goons all around us. No Slippin' had created a nice fan base all around the city. We were doing shows and bringing acts in like clockwork, did three shows with Cash Money's Little Wayne in Pittsburgh, Baltimore, and Philly. We lost out in Baltimore because our promoter got out on us by not advertising as he said he did. Bumps and bruises from being new to the industry of hiring acts and a venue away from Pittsburgh, I guess.

I met Little Wayne the first time in 2001 when he didn't even have dreadlocks yet. Maine, Pa, and Fifty Gs were creating a nice buzz. We had hit after hit that had catchy hooks like, "What Happened to That Boy" and "Hop in The Cadillac" or "Ain't Nothing U Can Do About It", which was the featured album title.

We spent time in Atlanta with Big Roe and Lou from New Orleans making music. I bounced around so much in 2001 trip after trip, state to state, city to city. I'd spend time in Philly with the Dominican connects during NBA All-Star break and Philly's annual festivals they would have. You might've caught me front row letting my fiancée flick it up with Don King during a De la Hoya vs Vargas fight in Vegas.

2001 flew past pretty fast, staying as busy as I was. By this time, I'm stacking fifty grand at a time just tucking it away. Spreading the wealth, though. I never left everything at just one spot. That way if the police ever came for me, they would never get everything I put my life on the line for. I enjoyed Atlanta so much I took one of my cars down there and left it in a storage spot.

Sleep If You Want To

One day in early December, we got a stretch of nice weather and the sun was shining. My fiancé, our daughter, and I hopped in the Navigator and headed out the Duke to handle something with wedding arrangements with my sister. So we got over there, I dropped them off at my sister's, and then called CY to see if they were up in the back by Seer's house chillin' as usual. When we were out that way nowadays since we stopped going to Swamps to gamble after ET passed away. He said they were, so I told him I'd be up after I stopped past Steph's to pick up some money. I got up there, pulled on the side of Seer's house, got out the truck and walked over to the front porch where CY was sitting. He let me know that Seer was inside with Bowie and some white boy taking care of something and smoking. So I sat on the step and rolled up a joint. Ten minutes later, Bowie and the white boy came out and didn't speak or anything, got into their Malibu and pulled off. Seer came out and we talked briefly about a few things and arranged something for the following day. We sat outside laughing and smoking for another twenty minutes before Monica called and said she'd be ready in an hour. I hung the phone up and the Malibu that Bowie was in pulled back up. He jumped out of the passenger side with a white towel wrapped around his hand with a long black banana clip hanging out the bottom. He ran up on me and pointed the gun into my chest and said, "Follow me, now. Follow me. Follow me now!" All I could do was just stand up and start back-peddling until I hit the screen door and opened it. Once I realized he wasn't going to shoot me at point-blank range, and that he had allowed me to stand and back away into the house, In complete shock. I started talking back. I said, "Alright. It's on now. You should have killed me, my man," and once he started walking to the car, I yelled, "Come back through. I got something for you!" By this time, CY had already dipped off and was going to the garage to grab one of the pistols we kept nearby just for a situation such as this. Sure enough, CY came back with it just a few seconds after the Malibu had pulled off. I grabbed the pistol and cocked it back making sure there was one in the chamber. To my disbelief, as I walked towards the truck, the Malibu hit the corner at the bottom of the hill and I immediately started blasting at it. At the same time, he was spitting a lot more rounds in my direction. I was leaning on the side of the truck, aimed and let off a couple more when I heard the sound of shattered glass and screeching tires. I looked over the truck and saw the Malibu back up in reverse fast. I couldn't believe it! My old roommate who I would have ride or died with at one point had pulled a gun on me and we had just tried to kill one another. His mother and my mother lived just blocks from one another. I had no idea what he was even talking about, follow him now!!! I hadn't followed him nor seen him since we were in the limo. The Malibu had a busted window and holes in it I'm sure. I now had to call Monica and let her know what had just happened. I wasn't going to drive that truck. I had money inside it, and it had two bullet holes in it. I wasn't going to put my daughter back in that truck and jeopardize running across him again on our way out. We rearranged some things and got home safe. I didn't hear the end of her mouth for quite some time about her truck until it was fixed. That was the last time I ever saw Bowie. Doc and Flash had been settled in down in ATL although they were still dipping and dabbling in the game. 2002 had rolled around almost time to get married, give up the game, buy a few more homes, and secure a major record deal.

UNLIMBER YOUR THINKING FROM ALL BONDAGE! GOD DOESN'T BUILD WITH HEWN STONES...THE SOUNDS OF MENS TOOLS HAMMERING DOWN ON MY CHILDREN IS AN OFFENSE TO ME YESTERDAYS VISION ONLY SPEAKS OF THE PAST AND NOT YOUR FUTURE!!!!!!!!!!!!!!! RELINQUISH THE PAST AND STEP OBEDIENTLY INTO THE NEXT PHASE ......THE FATHER SAID DO NOT LOOK BACK, RIGHT??????

Chapter Fifteen

So Glad I Made It

We were spoiled now. We fully controlled when and where we wanted our connect to meet us. Everybody had branched completely off into separate groups. We still hung out, partied, vacationed, and shared our new studio in the Strip District. I had just finished up a conversation with one of my drivers. She had said she experienced a close call on the turnpike after meeting one of the connects an hour and a half away from the 'Burgh. She said the state troopers pulled her over for going five miles per hour over the speed limit. She said she was in cruise control going 70 instead of 67 in a 65 zone, as I had instructed her to always do. According to her, the officer walked up, asked her why she was in a rush and asked her where she was coming from. Her reply was Seven Springs and to pull the bogus paperwork out we had fixed up to always be on point just for this reason. The only problem was she didn't have the paperwork. She forgot it on the couch at her home. The officer ran her license and registration, wrote her a ticket, and told her to slow down. She must've not fit the PROFILE, drug dealer description because he didn't pull the dog out and ask to search the vehicle the way they had done my other driver when she was stopped for speeding after dropping some money off to the connect a few months before. She didn't have the complexion for the connection as did this driver. This driver that was merely given a ticket was a middle-aged white lady that was married with two little kids. So that whole thing about the police stereotyping certain individuals from specific backgrounds is true. They had let a major, major package through, over two thousand bundles. I heard that story and just stood in shock like, wow it could have been over that fast! I was so happy she made it. I knew if she ever got caught, she would tell. Her husband never knew about her second job as a runner.

Everything was finalized with the wedding and there were just a few months left before the big day. One of the last things to do would be to get the invitations out with a return RSVP so we could finalize our count. Monica was getting ready to have them sent out and I happened to request for her not to include our home address on the cards. We already had a PO Box, so I told her to use that for the returns. Well, she didn't hear or didn't listen to me. One way or the other, she sent all the invitations out with our home address on it! That was the mistake I tried so desperately to avoid by all means! No Slippin'!

On no level did I like to slip. Three weeks after the invitations went out, I was out handling some business and I got a call from her saying the Allegheny

County Police had just left our house. “They found a bag of money and the new pistol you had in the box,” she cried out to me. First of all, I knew that the County Task Force didn’t typically do raids on city homes. They usually stayed in the surrounding areas outside of city limits. Secondly, the warrant to search sounded fishy once I read it. They claimed that somebody, a “CS” had just been to my home 48 hours prior and saw a big duffle bag full of heroin and that I was selling drugs out of my home. That was an absolute lie because I never brought the business into my home and I knew my circle was way tighter than that. I was brainstorming, though. I was going to find out who had sent them if anyone did.

One person came to mind at first then I ruled him out because he had only got caught with two ounces of weed. But Tone B was on the radar for about an hour ‘til I went to his home and talked to him. I had just bonded him out from jail a few days prior because the County Task Force ran up in his home and found almost 200 bricks that I had fronted him. He had just got with me about a month before since Doc Boog and Flash had accused him of something and had some sort of falling out with him. I had just started giving him stuff and this happened. So we sat and talked, and he said they had taken some of his mail and that he noticed they took the envelope with my wedding invitation and RSVP. Then I put two and two together and came up with they made up a bogus warrant from that. But they wanted me to think it was Tone B and I'd try to do something to him. Well, I knew better; Tone B was a stand-up guy. We had been on missions before together and he knew the code. He also knew I would make sure he was alright just as I did. I paid for his lawyer and his bond after he had just got caught with $40,000 worth of business. Yes, between that $40,000 he owed me and the $64,000 they took out of my house, I had just lost over $100,000 plus his bond and his lawyer fees.

The very next day, I had some people pack us up and we moved to an upscale luxury townhome community and didn't use not one bill or car or anything with that address. I hired a lawyer for advice and to see what was up, if I had a warrant for the money and gun or what. The gun wasn't stolen so there wasn't anything they could do about that, but the money concerned me because of the amount. But to my surprise, I didn't have a warrant or anything. I put Tone B back on and let him do his thing the very best way he could, considering the circumstances. I changed my phone numbers and phones also after that happened. So when I saw everyone that worked for me, I reconnected in person and gave my NEW number back out!!!!!!!!

About a week after that, we were downtown shopping at Mo Gear for the trip out to Cali that we were leaving for the next day. From the store, I saw my old head riding pass in his candy apple red Cadillac convertible with his newly re-done piped out red and white plush interior. I flagged him down and said what's up. He said he had tried calling me just the day before, but my phone was off. I told him I had a new number and told him to meet me at the outback steakhouse inside PNC Park on the north side. We met, talked about business, and got on with our day. He had told us how some big Coke Boys on the Northside where he was from had got indicted the week before and they were all telling on each other because they were facing life sentences and that two of them were his family members. He also said he needed me to give him more than usual because the business had picked up since that happened. That was perfect because I wanted to recoup that $100,000 I loss and the wedding was in two months.

Here it is June 2002 and my whole No Slippin' Records team and I, along with my fiancé, were headed out to LA for the 2nd Annual BET Awards. We had all our things for promotions and our agenda right along with us. We had reserved our rooms at the Kodak Theater months ahead of time. So when we arrived, our presence was felt! We had all our artists wear No Slippins t-shirts and they were instructed to pass out snippets and flyers. Free, from 106 and Park, stopped me and wanted to know who I was and where we were from. I had my yellow Pirate Jersey on with my black and yellow Pirates hat along with my Jacob big face watch. I had gone to New York City and personally got it from Jacob himself. I experienced the whole getting locked in his store and going upstairs sipping the finest wine while the sale was pending. I also had on the platinum chains with our logo and all. Oh, I can't leave out the golf ball diamond earrings to match. I grabbed Free's attention while the homies video recorded it. It was all good until my fiancé walked out of the glass doors with Foxy Brown. She came and handed me a camera and asked me to take a picture of them. I was pissed. That threw my whole conversation off and another thing was they should've been asking to take a picture with me, not handing me a camera!

I had Big Dee with me. He was one of our four managers and he had the gift of gab for sure. I came down into the lobby one time and he was sitting there drinking and talking to Slim, one of the Cash Money owners you never see on TV. He was tall, like almost 7 foot and looked like he could've been a hoop star. Everybody had their jersey's on. Baby, who was also standing nearby, had his John Elway throwback on. They remembered and knew us from the shows we booked with them a while before.

On the day of the event, we were on the red carpet feeling like rock stars. I was determined to make something happen. We partied with all the stars all week long. During the actual show, we sat up high near a rear door and to our complete surprise before Cash Money's performance, they came and sat right where we were. We added a few more resources while out there networking. We walked up into Sony and Universal not knowing who we were looking for. We didn't get any further than the receptionist, but it was worth a try and we dropped off music with her.

I called Gadgey up while I was out there hoping he could come and get us right on some smoke the first day, but he said he was living a few hours away. He did make a phone call to get us right, though. His boy called me and told me to stay on the phone with him while he directed us to him. That was an experience itself. We got to him, grabbed an ounce of some purple haze and were on our way back out. He told us whatever we did, do not turn onto some street one light over because they set trip and will probably shoot the car up if they saw us riding down their street. So once again, he stayed on the phone with us and directed us out pretty easily.

On the flight back, my new puppy Zeus was on my mind. Zeus was a Presco Canario Spanish Terrier. I had gone to this spot in Atlanta and met Art the owner of Premier K-9. He was the truth. He had Mike Tyson's rottweilers on his grounds. The R&B singer Monica was there, and we picked puppies from the same litter. When I got back to Pittsburgh, everyone couldn't understand how big he was. He was super strong. And his mouth was like a gator's mouth. Art had sent a video back with Zeus and encouraged my fiancée and me to watch it and stay on top of Zeus because he would try to bully us, as he was the ultimate protective dog breed. As a puppy, he could stand up and look me in the eyes as an 8-month old puppy. I was the first to introduce Presa Canario's to Pittsburgh. Everyone had American Terriers. They had known nothing about the dominate, beautiful breed of terriers from Spain. That was my boy, Zeus. When we got back, I went to pick him up from my mom's and she pleaded with me to let her keep Zeus. She fell in love with him in those couple of days that we were in Cali. Monica didn't mind. She was afraid of Zeus and afraid to have our daughter around him. So I ended up giving Zeus to my mother.

The wedding day rolled around and I was happy, nervous, and relieved that I had made it this far. I had the closest men to me at the time participating in my wedding. My old head, which was her uncle, my brother, CY, Rook, Tee, Tone B, my son, my nephews, and my beautiful girls as flower girls. If my cousin Reub wasn't still on the run, he would've been in it. Here it was years later, and he was still hiding out. Monica had gone all out. We were married in Oakland, PA at a very large church next to the University of Pittsburgh main campus. She ordered a dove release followed by a horse-drawn carriage that took us on to the perfect setting to take photos.

Once we arrived at the reception, I was quite proud of the great work she had orchestrated.

Everything was detailed and right on point from WAMO'S hottest DJ at the time to the camera crew, ice sculptures, family and friends. God had blessed me again and put the perfect woman in my life at the right time and in which probably had saved me from life in prison to becoming a victim of what the hood had to offer had I stayed in the hood much longer! I was ready to slow down a little bit, things were evident by the huge step I had just taken and tied the knot. So I thought!

To fuel the costs that were being incurred for our music, our artists and staff, the company vehicles and their living expenses, we had to keep hustling because we had got overhead with the celebrity lifestyle. We had to pay to play. I had passed the ball slowly after constantly getting on CY and T for not stepping up to the plate with the business. CY wanted to wait and let me orchestrate everything. I guess he was pretty much still under my umbrella. He was comfortable in that position, I guess. Rook had stepped up big time though and was handling things. Tee always just wanted to put his money up for the music but didn't want to invest in the traveling time and promotional part of it.

As far as the street business went, I told them all the same thing all the time, "Don't keep waiting on me to make the call, arrange everything, and do everything all the time." Tee and I got into a little physical altercation the night we had Little Flip in town because he didn't want to help. Just wanted to sit like he's the

Mayor of the City and politic and gossip about the latest hood happenings, staying in touch with every hood. After the reception the following morning, we were off for a trip to Florida to board a cruise ship and set sail for a weeklong honeymoon. Wifey had our baby girl so spoiled that she talked me into bringing our daughter and paying for our second babysitter to come along to watch her.

Once we got back, I had a ton of business to take care of. The first thing was while I was away, Tim from NYC had called me and said he shopped our music around and connected with a high-power entertainment attorney in New York and we needed to meet with him when I got back. So we arranged that meeting and was all loaded up in the small 7 passenger minivan. Tee, CY, and I had pitched in $5,000 each just in case the attorney wanted some change as a retainer fee. Better to always be prepared than unprepared.

Our designated driver was behind the wheel. We left the city and hit the turnpike. We hadn't even gotten five miles down the road and a state trooper pulled us over. Courtney had seen them behind us from the time we jumped on the turnpike. They were right at the entrance as if they were waiting for us to get on the highway. The trooper pulled us over and immediately got out with the K-9 and told us not to move as he called for backup. It was clear that this wasn't about a traffic violation; this seemed personal instead. He didn't ask many questions and surely wasn't pleasant in answering any questions we asked either. The K-9 wasn't hitting on anything, but the officer wouldn't let up. They pulled our bags we had in the back out, laid them on the ground and started searching them. Eventually, they found the $15,000 cash we had for the attorney. They confiscated the cash then let us go. It was really strange how they had just executed a completely illegal search! We still made the trip; we were just unprepared now.

Reub met up with us in New York and discussed his displeasure with Rodney about him being in the way and a rumor that started floating around amongst his little homies that got back to Reub. Rodney had expressed his desire to Rob me or my cousin Mo. Mo was moving things for Reub. Me, I wasn't one bit worried about him ever attempting to rob me on any level. I stayed ready. But it did piss me off! And I planned on addressing the issue sooner rather than later. But right now, I was trying to get my wife to move to Atlanta. Big homie L had a plug on brand new half a million-dollar homes that I was ready to get up into. Wifey made every excuse in the book not to follow through on that move, though.

In the meantime, we were planning to put $50,000 up each to promote a Roy Jones Jr. fight. Options and avenues were unlimited for the kid from Cochrandale projects deep inside the game. I invested in a clothing business with Hassan, Doc Boog, and

Flash at a mall on the outskirts of Atlanta. Big L was making calls trying to get No Slippin' plugged in with a tycoon in the industry. I was in and out, on and off.

Once I got back from ATL, Reub was back in town. He was trying to catch up with Rodney. Rodney had taken something off of Mo. I was way over the situation now. I called Mo and asked for Rodney's number and I immediately called him. The boy picks the phone up with a tough tone of voice, I ask why he had run off with that package. He came back over the other end of the phone and said, "Come get it, then," I told him alright that I would have him dealt with in a matter of time, hung up, called Mo back demanding to know where Rodney was staying. What he was driving and all the specifics? I said some very explicit comments over the phone before I finished up the conversation with Mo. I called Reub back and we went from there.

Rook called me and was saying the last package wasn't on point and he thinks it has to be sent back up there for re-packaging. I hung up with him and Shon was calling saying the same thing. I got quite a few callbacks from all my peoples, which created unnecessary talking over the phones. I called the plug and told them they had to come and get what was left. But before they had even come, we had our other plug on his way into town the day of the Super Bowl.

The day before the Super Bowl, I had left from CY's house with some money and was headed home, as I noticed what seemed to be a couple of cars following me. They were swerving in and out of traffic just as I was doing. That was obvious that something wasn't right. I wasn't just 'high' being paranoid, someone was following me. I dipped in and out of traffic until I had lost the vehicles that were behind me. Then I saw red and blue lights appear in an instant. I pulled over and thought to myself, "Got d**n it! This is it. I'm about to lose another $25,000!" The officer walked up, shined the light into the car, and asked for my license. I gave it to him, as he glanced and handed it back. He walked away while on his cell phone returned and said, "Alright. Slow down. You can't be in that much of a hurry. Slow down."

When I got home and told wifey the story, she said, "Baby they let you go because they must have a D.N.T on you. They just wanted to make sure that was you they were following." *Why would they have a do not touch order on me?* I couldn't believe he didn't ask to search or didn't even give me a speeding ticket. After it soaked in half the night, I agreed that her theory was likely true. But why?

The next day came around with it being Super Bowl Sunday. It was like I had forgotten all about what had taken place the night before. CY was hosting a party at his house, that way we would get to the connect easily when they got off the turnpike to the hotel, we told them to come to. When they got to the hotel, they would call and give the room number. We had already lined everyone up to be ready to get theirs whether the game was on or not. We planned to get it and distribute it before the game even came on. I called Reub and told him where to come, too. Rook was on standby along with my other cousin, Steph. They called while I was already in route to CY house, so I just turned around and went straight to the hotel. I let CY know the room number and that was that. Shon, CY's brother, had called and asked if he could get in on the boat. I told him he had to holla at his brother about that.

I pulled up at the hotel, circled the hotel making sure nothing seemed suspicious. Everything looked good so I parked and walked towards the front entrance. I hit the lobby and went straight to the elevator. Once I got off on the 7th floor everything looked good, so I hit door 723 with a light tap, tap. Teko answered the door and smiled, "Hey my friend." I nodded, then locked the top latch on the door. We started talking for a minute before we heard a knock on the door. I thought it was Reub or CY, but it wasn't, it was a cop!

My heart sunk. I turned and ran toward the window thinking I was going to jump, but by then they had already hit the door with a battering ram and knocked it clean off its hinges. They had guns drawn and quickly handcuffed us and escorted us to another room across the hall. A couple of minutes later, they came over the walkie talkie and said two more are in custody. They brought CY and Courtney in the room, also. Here we are holed up in the presence of a room full of undercover police officers. They didn't have any drugs at the time. They did confiscate the money we had on us, which wasn't that much; it wasn't near enough to cover the kilogram of heroin the Dominicans had stashed in the vehicle's secret compartment. They couldn't find the drugs in that car at first, so they took us downtown to the DEA building. That's when I knew it was the FED's who had busted us. They didn't reveal any information to us except that they had a kilo of heroin in the vehicle and that we all were in trouble and facing a lot of time. They asked if we had anything, we wanted to let them know, we all declined and got processed.

We sat in different rooms for a couple of hours before they suddenly opened the doors, handed us some paperwork and our cell phones, and released us! They kept the Dominicans, though. Reub had said that he pulled up at the hotel and seen all the undercover police cars out front and I didn't answer my phone, so he left. He was lucky he had just somehow slipped through the cracks then.

I got out in front of the DEA building and turned my phone on. I had so many calls and messages from my wife. Nearly message after message text after text was from her. They had confiscated a couple of phones I had on me. I called my wife and told her to come to pick me up, and that I would explain when I saw her. I knew one thing for sure: I was going to see my lawyer when the sun came back up first thing Monday morning.

I couldn't sleep for the whole night. I tossed and I turned. That was a Super Bowl that I would never forget! I went and saw my attorney that Monday along with the paperwork I had as he listened to the story I told him. His reply was, "Let me call him. I know him. He will tell me what they have on ya'll." He called right in front of me and conversed as if they were next-door neighbors. They probably were. He hung up the phone and said, "Clabo, I have good news and bad news. Which do you want first?"

Wymard went on to say, "The way they do things, they don't come unless they have something concrete on you that'll stick." He said that if he was me, he would first go clean everything up and stop whatever I was doing. He said anything that I want to keep, I'd better hide it well. Any jewelry, cars, money, etc. they will be coming to confiscate anything that they could get their hands-on, including paperwork. Wymard said, "They will be back once they wrap up and unseal the indictments in a week or two. And throw your phones away. Didn't you hear about the massive cocaine ring they just indicted on the Northside? They seized millions of dollars. It was unbelievable and I hear that they have another one stemming from that. You didn't mess with those guys, did you?" I said, "No, no, not at all," but in the back of my mind, I thought about my old head, Uncle Mike. I asked what he would charge to represent me. He said $5000 would retain him, but it'll probably be between 25 to 35 thousand dollars total. I agreed and gave him the $5000 on the spot without doing my homework and not realizing that just because he's a beast in state courts with homicide and drug offenses that doesn't mean he's a beast on the federal level!

I had retained him for Reub already, so I was familiar with his experience in beating drug and homicide cases. I was very confident in his work, just as I was confident in Mark Lancaster, but Lancaster was still fairly new and young, so I just thought retaining the most popular defense attorney in the City was the way to go. We shook hands and the wife, and I was on our way.

We left out the building. I had her immediately call Uncle Mike to see if he was around. He answered and said he was home, so we stopped over. I told him my story of what had happened to me and then he starts telling me some things saying he got pulled over down in Manchester a couple of months ago and the DEA took $50,000 cash off of him! I was pissed off that he didn't tell me that way back when that happened to him. I asked for the money that he owed me and told him I was done. The game was over.

We left his house, got in the truck and had a silent ride home. Before we got back out, I looked over my shoulder, kissed my wife and told her, "I promise you everything will work out. You won't have to worry or need or want for anything. Just stay strong and take care of my baby girl."

We put two and two together and realized that they had probably got on me from Uncle Mike. We cleaned everything, tightened everything up, had everything in order and on point and just spent as much time as possible together. Going on the run wasn't even a thought. No way in the world would I leave my family and my children in that position. All I could do was prepare myself the best way I could. I collected everything I could without being on the phones. The only person I didn't catch up to was Hoody. The same one who I was about to handle, but Rook saved a while before due to my cousin Twan's situation. And here it is, he avoided running that money in on time.

A few days later at about 5:30 am I heard the cars pulling up in the driveway. I jumped up, woke my wife up and told her, "That's it, baby. They're here." I started to head downstairs after the first knock, but the first knock was followed by a boom just like at the hotel the day of the Super Bowl. They knocked the door down and threw me to the floor. They tore the house up. They kept asking where the money and the fancy jewelry was. They only got my earrings and a few thousand dollars. They took my wife's wedding ring, but for some reason, they didn't take my wedding band off my finger. Somehow, they missed it. Not sure how when it was platinum with four and a half-carat baguette invisible set. Well, I did manage to turn it to the inside of my hand after I was sitting on the floor a while. I thought for sure they'd take it once I got arraigned, but they didn't. They took her truck but left the other two little low-key runner cars in the driveway. They asked where my jaguar was. I told them I had no idea what they were talking about. I told them to run my name; I don't own any vehicles. I don't have a car in my name. They then went into saying we had thirty minutes for someone to get to the house to get our daughter or she was going to CYS. The reason being was because they were arresting my wife also! They said she was being indicted for aiding and abetting. That was a complete shock! Talk about the element of surprise. I had no idea what they were talking about. I didn't allow her to even know much anymore, let alone touch anything!

Thank God that my mother-in-law answered the phone and made it out there by the time they were ready to leave. My world was tumbling upside down. My daughter was 2 ½ years old, so she had no idea what was going on. All I can see is the look on my innocent baby's face filled with confusion and tears. They put me in one car and my wife in another.

On the ride downtown in the unmarked DEA car with dark tinted windows, the officer says, “So, what’s up? You wanna talk? Listen, I’ll tell you this. You’re up here at the tip-top now. You talk to us; you’ll be at the bottom.” I declined his offer and said, “Talk to my lawyer.” His phone rang. He picked it up and started listening as the person on the other end started talking. I heard the cop say, “You got ‘em all? Good!”

This time we didn’t go to the DEA building. He pulled up at the ACJ instead. Soon as I got through the doors, I noticed a holding tank full of people I knew. All my homies. Well, a few anyhow. Me, my wife, CY, his brother Shon, Courtney, and my cousin Steph. They had my old head in a holding tank across from us with a bunch of other people. I only recognized one though. He happened to be with my old head one day when I was buying three kilos of coke off my old head. Come to find out, he was one of the big boys on the Northside.

It was soon revealed that they had intercepted over a thousand phone calls from various phones we had. Courtney had never been in any trouble and he wasn’t a street person. He just got caught up with being one of our designated drivers, so his cooperating was likely.

Everyone ended up making bond after a marathon of hearings that was put on by the US Attorney to detain us. I was very happy when I found out my wife was released. I knew she was a soldier and would do as I thought she would. Steph wasn't a street person. He only got in the game after having his football dreams cut short due to a leg injury his senior year in college. He just happened to want to live the lifestyle because he saw the fast money.

The two Dominican's were still in the ACJ on the same block as my homie Tone B. With the courtroom jam-packed with attorneys, co-defendants, media personnel, family and friends, one by one Judge Conti allowed my co-defendants to go free on bond. Me on the other hand, my time before the judge was different. The US Attorney stunned the entire courtroom when they started playing phone recordings. They were trying to convince the judge that I was a menace to society; that I was ordering people to be robbed, shot, and killed. They played the conversation where I was on the phone with Mo asking him about Rodney's home and his whereabouts followed by another call to Rodney when I threatened his life. They said that they had to set up surveillance around Rodney's home and his mother's home for almost three weeks until I was arrested. They played another conversation with me talking to my cousin Reub. They said he had been on the run for a homicide charge for over three years and that I harbored a fugitive for that entire time. They argued that if I was released, I would most likely flee from justice. They went on to say that more indictments would follow as this was only the beginning of the investigation. They claimed a superseding indictment was likely and more arrests were pending in and around different cities and states. Conti agreed with their request by saying that she was disturbed by the phone calls and that she wouldn't sleep at night if she placed me back into society. The ACJ became my new home.

Here I was twenty-six years old and the streets had finally caught up to me after fifteen years since I sold my first drug. My first attorney visit was a little disturbing. Wymard had come over and said he would file an appeal to get back in for another detention hearing, but the chances looked slim. He mentioned that they were possibly going to do a superseding indictment and charge me in New York and Philadelphia also. He said that he had heard Doc Boog and Flash were about to be indicted, also. He said that he heard that a runner got caught on the turnpike with over a quarter of a million dollars and they cooperated and implicated them. Well, I knew that part was true because CY had told me that his girlfriend told him that.

Wymard continued to say that all of my co-defendants are cooperating and had already been meeting with the DEA since they've been out. He said their attorneys would not go into detail about what they had told the DEA, but that I was the last man standing, besides Riz and CY's brother.

I was so angry with everyone at this point. Cuz had me pay for his attorney, then he did that to me! CY and I pitched in on Courtney's lawyer and he had done this to me?!? I didn't quite know what to expect from him, so I was somewhat surprised that he had started talking to them. *At least he didn't know where I stashed my money.*

Rook held me down and he was there every step of the way. He even met the guards on the outside so I could smoke good green while I was in the ACJ. Yes, I stayed high every day in there. I hired Mark Lancaster to represent my wife. The next time Wymard came to see me he said the DEA contacted him and told him if I didn't cooperate that they were going to charge my mother and sister with money laundering and they were going to add additional charges onto my wife and were re-arresting me on attempted murder for hire charges, racketeering and a superseding indictment would soon follow. *Things had just got real.* I stared at Wymard like *what the hell. I paid you $30,000 to just talk to the police for me??? What are you going to d*o? "What do you have in your arsenal to beat these charges? What angle are you fighting from?!" I inquired. He couldn't give me any explanation whatsoever. I ended the visit immediately and went back on the block.

Tone B. was on 6E block with me, so I told him exactly what the attorney had just said. His response, "Do whatever you gotta do, Dog. They offered me ten years already I'm taking it.'' I called CY later that afternoon He answered and said, "I am not allowed to talk to you, Dog!" and hung up the phone! He must have been scared of the bond conditions or was it because of his conscience from being debriefed? It was a question I'd ask myself over the next few nights in the cell.

Riz and Shon were on state parole already, so I didn't get a chance to talk with them. They were immediately sent back upstate. I was concerned that they were trying to still hold surveillance to see where I had my money. So I put everything on hold. I had my wife reach out to Tee to handle something for me temporarily until the smoke cleared and he wouldn't take her calls. Tee avoided me and my wife. The only reliable person was Rook; no matter what he made things happen. He did whatever I asked.

A few days later, Tone B. got off the phone and walked into my cell and said, "Dog, they just picked up Flash and Doc and a few other boys." I looked and said, "I told you, bro, what Wymard said! They probably coming to re-arrest me, too!" I got on the phone and called my wife. I told her what happened and told her to have Lancaster and Wymard come see me together at the same time.

As we were watching the evening news the following night, Nitty comes walking through with his care bag. Things were getting strange now! On top of that, some kid from the Northside calls me and Tone B. to the cell and says Little Marv wants to talk to ya'll through the toilets. We looked at each other and went in. I walked in but didn't want to talk. I didn't have anything to say and certainly didn't want to hear anything. However, I was curious to know why Nitty was on the block. I saw fear in his eyes for the first time once he realized there were two Duke Boys on the block. We had the smoke, so we pretty much had the block on lock.

China Man was my celly and he knew all the young lunatics on the block from the Northside who was about that business. Nitty talked loud so it soon became known that he had just been indicted and brought down from the state jail where he was serving time for a parole violation.

A couple of days later, Lancaster and Wymard came to see me and gave me an update on what things were looking like. And from the sound of it, it wasn't looking good. They had indicted Crump and a few other people along with another one of our drivers. For Crump having graduated from Duquesne University, he still didn't seem to be the brightest bulb in the bunch. A few months after he made bond, the streets were saying that he was cooperating. Not only were the streets saying this, the attorneys were, also. So he made the statement to someone after he was spotted leaving the DEA building that he wasn't cooperating. He just had to go get debriefed! I laughed so hard when I heard that. *This college-educated guy didn't know what debriefed meant.* He self-surrendered and got a few months in a camp.

I was so shocked at the fact that when I received my paperwork, there were reports and statements from CS1 through CS8. According to the paperwork, CS3 used to live in New York, had multiple arrests in New York, and had just got like 60 months for drugs and a gun. After going through each CS and everything about them, which the government had to disclose, I realized it was Sheenie. Sheenie was one of Reub's workers at one point. I had never in my life dealt with this dirtball from New York. He made up a complete lie on me a year before this happened to me. The government allowed this slimeball to make up a story that had zero authenticity or truth at all. This snake from New York threw salt in the game and put heat on my name way before. I nor any of my homies would ever deal with him on any level. It was his little friend B's that I was going to deal with a long time ago. It's a dirty game. Another snake in the grass!

What Is Happening

I'm watching the news while I'm sitting at the chess table because the block went silent. There was a chase that ended on the Braddock-Rankin bridge. Reub and Rodney's faces were plastered on the screen. They said they arrested a fugitive that evaded the FBI and local municipalities for over three years along with another convicted felon. I couldn't believe it. My cuz was with Rodney! *Was he about to get him or something?* I couldn't understand why they were together. Cuz knew better than to even be running around over there. I guess things changed the day I was no longer there and able to make sure everything and everybody was alright. They put cuz on another block, but we managed to meet at church in the county jail. Rodney eventually got out of jail and was murdered one night in the City.

The government split Doc Boog and Flash up and started moving people around. Nitty got into it with my celly China Man one afternoon. He was mad because we wouldn't give him any smoke. So he and China Man had some words. We're sitting in our cell one-day smoking, Nitty ran up in our cell with a homemade knife in his hand. China grabbed his arm and I grabbed him from the back. Nitty was like 6'3 or 6'4 and in tip-top shape. We tussled and tussled, I knocked the shank down and kicked it underneath the bed. By that time, a crowd had gathered, and the guard eventually walked up to us. Oh yeah, some guards don't care. They let you get it on or whatever. As long as you're not bothering them, they will turn a blind eye if they don't like you. The funny part about this was, we all got locked down, the whole block.

We had his knife in our cell now. So China Man screams out, "A yo Nitty!" Nitty looks out his cell window on the door and says, "Yo, what up?" China Man says, "Aye, yo. You forgot something down here, Wody," and the whole block started laughing. Nitty says, "Oh yeah. Is that right?" China Man says, "Yes. Absolutely."

Nitty calls the correctional officer to his cell. They talk through the door for a minute. The C.O. go gets on the phone at his booth then says on the intercom, "Nitty, pack it up. You're being moved." On the way out as he was leaving, he started laughing saying he would catch up with us. Everybody laughed and clowned him as he left the block with everything wrapped inside his blanket tied in a knot.

Wymard soon came with some more information. Big Homie and Nitty had turned into government witnesses. I ended up cooperating after I negotiated an agreement that would save my wife from any federal prison time; no money laundering charges against my mother or sister or any immediate family member; I wouldn't face any additional charges on any superseding indictment down the road; and I would get immunity on murder for hire or whatever else they were planning on charging me with. They had over 1,000 conversations where we were discussing deals and referencing them as CDs or NFL jersey numbers. They had us! What part didn't they understand?

Once CY found out his brother was going to trial, he recanted his statements and pled guilty and was sentenced to ten years. They proceeded with the trial. I couldn't believe it. I'm sure nobody in Pittsburgh could believe Clabo was about to get funky in federal court. How fast my life had changed. I went from enforcing street codes and having everyone around me take the pledge to No Slippin' to trying to make it to the biggest stage of them all. I had visions of selling out arenas and possibly placing a Grammy on my mother's shelf along with the baseball trophies and plaques. Now I was getting on the stand in front of a jury and my community and telling a recorded conversation that was true. Never say never because you never know until you're faced with a situation that you never thought would happen and never had a vision of it happening in real-time when you least expect it. That first day I agreed to cooperate, I was putting my family, my mother, my sister, and my wife and several others out of the fire. They didn't ask to be a part of any of that. At the very same time, I was endangering them, also. The government offered to move my family before and after the trial was over. We all declined. My mother was well-known and respected in the Duke. She had answered her call to ministry and was preaching sermons. So you know she wasn't scared. She had on the armor of God and was filled with the Holy Spirit.

In between time, they had several phone numbers off of one of the burner phones with conversations with some of my other homies that they couldn't identify, and they played them over and over to me. Heck, as much as I stayed high, I couldn't remember who sounded like what to identify them either. I stuck to that story time after time. There were about a half dozen homies they couldn't identify and trust me they respect and remember and know they would've been booked if I was 'ratting'. I didn't and don't call it ratting. I call it being a man and being willing to die in prison at that time to save my family from the humiliation and life-altering federal convictions. Besides I let everyone know they could see me when I got out its whatever, about my family that's the definition of Family Over Everything.

My sister had gone to college and earned her degree while being a mother to four little boys at the time. I couldn't imagine or live with myself looking at her everyday knowing I messed her career up, tarnished her image, and put her in an even worse situation then she was already in having to be a single mom to four boys. No way in the world was I going to let them charge her with anything if I could stop it. I did stop it!

I still looked out for Riz, too. He could have been found guilty for way more than what they found him guilty of. Shon was on recording after recording and involved in multiple conversations. He was on the calls from Super Bowl night. I don't understand what they were thinking. There were hundreds of calls with each of my co-defendants over four-months. They should've respected me enough to not even go to trial like that. I made it very clear what was at stake. I was hurt, embarrassed, and worried about my family every single day. Not from anyone who I had looked out for before my incarceration, but from some young goon trying to make a name for himself or something.

Chapter Sixteen

Charge That to the Game

I was sentenced to 140 months, 11 ½ years, in federal prison. My wife received one day in federal custody. My mother was never charged nor was my sister or brother. Rook had slipped through, also. He was one of the homies that they couldn't identify early on but had asked on more than five different debriefings who that voice was. I'd always say I can't recognize it, I don't remember, etc. I sat in the county jail for about ten days after I was sentenced before the US Marshals came and picked me up to be transported to the prison facility where I would be housed. I got on the van for the ride out to the airport to board the federal plane they transport inmates on and Doc Boog is on the van saying he's headed back to Philly or something. I asked what was up with Flash, he says he doesn't know, but he better not wait 'til it's too late. *What do you mean by that Doc?* We talked until I got loaded on the plane. Being handcuffed and shackled on a plane is the most uncomfortable situation ever. Can you imagine seeing nothing but water then suddenly landing just beyond the water? That's what happened when the US Marshalls landed the plane somewhere in the sticks. This particular day, I ended up in Oklahoma to be processed and designated to a prison. As a planeload was going into the federal holding facility, there was a line on the opposite side getting loaded onto the plane. Convicted felons from all over the world, mainly the United States, were being processed like animals on a farm. I sat quietly and observed and tried to block out the storytelling that goes on nonstop behind the walls. I was given a bagged lunch, asked a ton of questions, and was so happy when I got a cell and a three-inch-thick mattress to lay down on. I figured my wife would be concerned so I decided to call the following day once I got up, but I waited and when I finally got through, she was crying on the other end. She had broken down and said she just misses me so much and that my children were asking where I was. I thanked her for still taking the time out to get my other two children and tried to reassure her that everything would be alright. She was also worried about my well-being. Again, I assured her that I would do my best to be safe and make good decisions. We both didn't quite know what to expect. But I knew for sure I wasn't going into this alone. I had my wife one hundred percent with me, and God was guiding me every step of the way. I had hit rock bottom emotionally and was feeling anxiety, depression, and unknown thoughts. Where am I getting sent to? When would I get there? Who will I see? Would I have to stab someone? Or would someone attempt to stab me? I had heard plenty of stories but living it was a whole different thing. I still wasn't trusting God fully because if I was,

I wouldn't be so uneasy and concerned with the unknown.

Lonely on Lockdown

I ended up at FCI Gilmer in West Virginia. Once that bus finally pulled into the prison it was dark. Everyone was processed and being called and assigned to their blocks. I happened to be the next to the last inmate called. Eventually, I was escorted to my designated block after being asked a series of questions of whether or not I had problems with certain individuals, specifically a couple of names I knew very well. One being CY! I said no and eventually was escorted to A block. I was ready to deal with him whatever way he wanted to handle it. Once on the block nearly everyone was on the doors looking out the windows from the cells. Everyone was locked down for the night. I heard a couple of inmates yelling, "Wow. They brought that boy Clabo up here. Wow!" It was evident they knew who I was, but I didn't recognize but one of them. Dank. The same kid that was Nitty's cellmate in the county jail that I had cursed out and threatened.

I ended up in a cell with someone that never rolled over out of his bunk, even to look and see or say anything. The follow morning after not hardly getting any sleep, I begin to hear doors clank open and the chatter began. My celly made some quick small talk only after I asked about the chow hall and timing. I went and grabbed me some breakfast and sat alone. After the meal, I was heading back to the block when someone called my name. I turned around and waited. He walked up and said, "What up, Dog. Let's talk. Keep walking, slow though. Ole boy big homie from the way wanna talk to you." I asked who it was and where he was at. He tells me, "On the next move, come down the steps and I'll be waiting on you."

Next move, I went down and he says, "Follow me, bro. Just walk straight past the guard." I got a little uneasy being I was now on another block! I followed him we go into a cell that had a towel over the window. Here we go. I don't have anything to protect myself except for the Holy Spirit. But having little to no fear, I go in and I'm standing between three boys from Pittsburgh, ole boy says, "Bro, I'mma keep it 100 with you. Ya boy CY was pressured to put some change up to deal with you from the situation with his bro. Bro, it's best that you just go to the guard and say somebody threatened you, but don't say my name or what I look like. If you stay here bro somebody is going to try and get at you. I know ya status bro from the streets, but that legacy got tarnished bro when you got on the stand. Bro, it'll be better if you just go in. All they gone do is transfer you in a couple weeks." He then stood up and gave me a handshake and said, "Just don't point me out when they show you pictures if you go."

I went back to my assigned block and thought about it for a couple of hours. During lunch, I was looking for CY hoping I would've seen him because I had my mind made up that I would've run up to him and we both would've been in the hole. God had another plan and it didn't involve those thoughts.

I went in and was placed in solitary confinement. They took my khaki-colored pants and top and replaced it with an orange jumpsuit. I was placed in a cell alone next door to MC, another felon from the Northside who I had known somewhat on a business level. He was telling the guard who came to investigate his write up that he is okay to go back into population and that someone had robbed his cell and took his sneakers and food. Another indication that this wasn't the streets because in the streets he had a reputation for putting in work. A couple of days later, I get some mail from the DEA stating that they were giving my house back to me, being it wasn't of value to them. They had seized the duplex in Duquesne, then after further evaluation decided they didn't want it. I was surprised, but not mad at all. It brought a little joy in a downtime. I had never heard of anything like that happening though. Attached was another letter. This was a forfeiture agreement for the 60 something thousand the county task force had taken from our home a couple of years earlier. I signed it and sent it back off.

A couple of days turned into weeks. I started receiving mail regularly with updates from my wife as just as I was sending them back out with updates and the necessary documentation needed to get her cleared to visit me being that co-defendants aren't allowed to visit with each other. She was cleared and made the first visit that we had actual contact with one another and seeing my baby girl for the first time was amazing. During the time with letters going back and forth between us before the visit, she had said that the word on the streets was that I got stabbed up pretty badly and was on life support. Maybe that was the story they told CY to make it sound good to get whatever the price was for that. I'm sure they knew he was soft anyhow and no doubt he'd pay regardless and not say or question otherwise anyhow. Furthermore, on that first visit, as I walked into the visiting area towards the guard to get my instructions for the visit, he pointed to an area that was taped off on the floor designated for disciplinary inmates with orange jumpsuits but the focus soon became the guy that was sitting right near the area. It was CY and his mother looking as if they had seen a ghost. My wife and I just busted out laughing as I made it clear, "Clabo isn't on life support and I'm not stabbed up baby!" making sure that he and his mother had heard me. God certainly had a way of working things out in my favor. I guess that was his plan whenever I was ready to once again take things into my own hands. Our visit was wonderful, and I was certainly reassured that I had made the right decision when I picked this lady to take me hand in hand.

I had made one thing known for sure that no matter what I wasn't checking into the hole again regardless of who I ran across or where I ended up! Before I was shipped out of FCI Gilmer, my mother sent me a quest study Bible. I dug so deep into it because it was easy to read and understand, and it had answers to every question my mind could conjure up. If I wasn't doing push-ups and exercising in the cell, I was reading my daily newspaper I received every day a day behind the calendar, or I was writing letters and studying the Word.

FCI Allenwood was my next home located in central PA. Same routine when I arrived there. The uneasy feeling was gone. I was prepared for whatever would come my way. And sure enough during the intake process, I was asked if I had a problem with the African Warrior! At the time, I didn't know who the African Warrior was. I told the guard I didn't know who the African Warrior was until he showed me a picture of Nitty! Then I said, "Oh no. I don't have a problem with him." *Oh boy. Here we go again!* The last time I had seen him was in the county jail when he ran up in our cell and dropped his homemade knife. So I knew it was about to be on once again on a whole different level. To my surprise, the first time I noticed him on the compound the following day, he hadn't even noticed me, but I saw him and contemplated whether I should jump on him right then, being that he was walking with a cast on his leg. I certainly had the upper hand now!

Back on the block I looked at the inmate list posted on the screen and noticed Len's name on it. I immediately went looking for him. He had got caught with a trunk full of guns and was doing a twenty-year sentence. He ran with my cousin Twan. He had looked out on that side of things as needed. I waited outside his block on the next move and was happy to see him as he was to see me, also. Finally, I ran across some family. Somebody who wasn't going to judge me and someone who I knew I could trust and someone who would show me all the INs and OUTs.

We walked the yard and talked for a couple of days straight. I was catching him up on everything that had happened in the streets since he had been in prison. I let him know that they kept playing tapes with several people I 'couldn't identify'. Rook is one of them. I told him the situation with the African Warrior, and he told me that dude was up here in Allenwood and almost got checked in by the Bloods from New York because he was set trippin' and starting nonsense. Claiming Blood being around the boys from New York then would go trying to roll with Pittsburgh and at times claiming to be a five percenter or something. He said he didn't like him, and we could get him if I wanted to!

Len's name was Yusef now, though. He had become a Muslim. So getting used to calling him Yusef instead of Len Dogg took a little time. So the first time the Warrior saw me with Yusef, he looked nervous and didn't say much except what's up. I wasn't trying to go to the hole for fighting or anything. I wanted to do my time out in population and didn't want to lose any of the good time I would supposedly get 54 days a year off for every twelve months without any misconduct or write-ups.

Well, I was soon battle-tested because after we had gone to the commissary on our way back the Warrior decided he was going to play Mr. Loudmouth and start running off at the mouth. Yusef got involved, which then drew a few of his Muslim brothers that were nearby. The cameras must've picked something up or somebody dropped a note on the incident because they came to the block and arrested me and took me to the hole and placed me under investigation. I was so pissed.

This is what made me say they don't care about you at all. They'd prefer that you fight amongst yourselves and kill each other because the next day I was on the door and heard them bringing someone down the hall. As just about everyone had done when a new visitor visited the dark and lonely place where interaction was very limited. Mentally only the strong survive in isolation. I've seen inmates scream and talk to themselves. I've seen inmates throw and wipe feces all over themselves and on their cell windows and doors. Even wait for a guard to open a cell door or slot for medication call or for the chow tray to be slid through the opening in the door only to have feces or urine thrown back through the slot. "Awwww, they wild as heck. They gone put me in here with dude?" that was the African Warrior's indirect plea to the guards for them not to put him in the cell with me here in the hole. But they didn't listen to his plea whatsoever.

One of the three guards that had escorted him to the cell where I was, called my name and said, "Turn around. Hands behind your back and out through the opening." That was how you had to get the cell door open; only by handcuffing up first. I cuffed up and he entered. We were now locked in the same cell, shower inside the cell, one steel stool cemented to the floor along with a small table to write on. A fluorescent light that stayed on twenty-four hours a day seven days a week sat above the top of the triple bunk bed's steel frame. *I know three people can't live here together. I wouldn't even get just one celly!* We both got uncuffed and he says "What up. What you gone do? You gon' jump on me or what? You can get me with one leg." I said, "Naw, I'm trying to get back on the compound but you gon' stop the craziness, though."

Our bunks were no more than fourteen inches apart. Can you imagine not being able to roll over in bed? That's exactly what it was. I slept on my back day in and day out. We courtesy flushed the toilets when we had to go. We put a sheet up covering the bunks when it was time for us to shower. This was the true meaning of sleeping with the enemy. There wasn't any in-between. Either one of us was going to kill the other inside this small cell or we were going to get along. My 140 months could have easily turned into a life sentence if I had acquired the mindset that the system tries to install when you become a convicted felon. There was no doubt at all that they placed us together to see if we would try to harm one another. Only the strong survive. Here I am locked inside a cell in isolation with another snake. All my life all I've been around is snakes. And I'm still faced with it deep inside Allenwood Federal Correctional Institution.

I knew Nitty was a lunatic from the days he would pop up at our apartment and from the incident at the county jail. I was ready, though. I slept with one eye open as I'm sure he did, also. I had the upper hand because I had the lower bunk. He had the middle bunk. So I could hear any move he made. I hardly got any sleep because he started telling story after story, one after another about everyone he knew and nearly everything he knew. He indirectly told me that he had cooperated with the DEA after they had wanted information on the package he stole through the white girl. He mentioned that he had given the young boys weapons in the Duke to get at Flash and ET. He said he purposely tried to manipulate their minds. It paid off because the young boys ran up on ET for no reason at all. Everything he said added up. He said he had wanted to get Bowie because Bowie went behind his back and met with his connect in Philly. He said Bowie fled to Atlanta before he could catch up with him, though.

Some of the stories he told me blew my mind. All that stuff he was talking on the compound a few days earlier certainly didn't parlay into the fact that he was now telling me all this personal stuff. If I was so much of a snitch or a rat, or whatever he called me out to be a couple of days before this, why was he confessing all his sins and telling me all of his business? He was telling me these things as if I was his confidant or his brother or something.

Three days later, he was gone from the hole. He went to the outside hospital to get his cast removed. About a week later I was released from the hole and put back into population. Seeing the African Warrior on the compound now it was just a mutual what's up or small talk about him asking what I thought this person or that person was going to do in court or once they were released. He would always ask what I thought Flash was going to do, which I found to be very strange. I'd always say I don't know.

Shake It Off

I got involved with the basketball league. I played on Yusef's team. Other than that, I spent most of my time playing chess and studying my Bible. With 300 minutes a month to use, I called home nearly every day for ten minutes. I had a very special wife at home. I'd see people angry after they dialed out and didn't get through to anyone. They'd hang the phone up and walk off upset. The whole time I was in prison there was not one single time my wife didn't answer the phone. I can guarantee there aren't many people who have been in prison that can say they experienced that. I got visits every two weeks, also. I didn't want her, along with our baby, to drive three hours away to see me, but she did faithfully. I can recall one visit when this guy from DC was sitting next to us and had his collar lifted around his neck. I explained to my wife why he was doing that. He was messing with a punk on the compound. He had chased this person around the prison every day. He was a black guy that had tattooed the white boy's name on his neck and was on the visit with what looked to be his wife and kids. That was so disgusting. I wondered why or how his wife or kids never noticed the tattoo or asked why he kept his collar up. When he was on the compound, he didn't have his collar up. That wife of his probably didn't have any idea of what he was doing inside the prison because he was hiding the tattoo from her.

Opening my newspaper one day after mail call I saw something that grabbed my attention. Bulivar Calcano and another Dominican were just sentenced to 18 months in prison for supplying me the heroin to distribute in Pittsburgh. I read that over and over saying to myself that this has to be a misprint. There is no way the connect that supplied me the product only got 18 months, pretty much time served, while I got 140 months! *This federal system is so knocked off, it needs to be reformed.* It is designed to penalize African Americans more harshly than anyone else. How is it even possible for them to get 10 years LESS than me? Less than all of my co-defendants and everyone else I'd heard of recently. It turned out that the government was the biggest snakes of all!

As if that wasn't enough to read and have on replay in my mind when I called home, I was told that my grandmother had passed away. I was heartbroken. That was my girl. I was her favorite. I hadn't heard her voice in a long time and hadn't seen her pretty face in forever. What was going on? I wouldn't be able to help bury my Gram. No final goodbye. Not one more look at Grandma Evelyn. *Why me? Why did you have to take Gram away from me?* To this very day, I still miss my Gram. Rest in Peace Evelyn Dent.

A couple of weeks after, Yusef and I were working out in the yard when my number was called over the speaker for an attorney-client visit. I'm like, who the heck is this. My attorney drove three hours away to visit me. *What's going on?* On a Wednesday afternoon, I'm headed to the visiting room. I get to the visiting room after being escorted there. There are two DEA agents in plain clothes greeting me with a smile as if they were my friends or something. With the experience I endured, I hated them.

Despite them giving the house back and my wife's wedding band, I still hated them. "Clabo, have a seat. We're going to make this quick. We have some tapes here. We drove three hours to see if you remember and recognize this person now that your deal is on this table ready to be thrown away. We already know who this is now. Numerous people have identified him. Now we just want to know if this is the person?" They lifted a picture of Rook and handed it to me. "This is who's on the tapes, isn't it? We already have a warrant for him." I said "Well, why did you come way up here to ask me. Ya'll can't be just poppin' up on me like this. Ya'll tryna get me killed in here?"

A bit sarcastic and dramatic, but I was trying to get my point across. I started making all kinds of excuses. "He's family. I can't talk about family. That's off the table. He didn't do anything." I still never fully admitted that it was him on the calls. I said, "Maybe so, but I can't tell the voice for sure." But I did make sure they booked Hoody since he got smart with my peoples after she saw him in a bar and said he wasn't running in what he owed me. I figured out his voice quickly. My memory came back real fast. And I don't have any regrets about it either. He can ask himself if that five-digit tag he refused to pay was worth it. I left that fake attorney visit as fast as possible and met with Yusef and told him that they had just come up here asking about Rook. I called home and got the word out ASAP and had Yusef do the same. I was sick about it. I love Rook like a brother. He was the only one out there still taking care of things and making sure everyone was alright. Besides, he had just done ten years.

Twenty-five months later, I had read numerous books and business magazines like INC 500 and others I had subscribed to. I would read the Pittsburgh newspaper I received daily from front to back and everything in between. Occasionally, I'd get spiritual letters and literature from Pastor Jones.

Chapter Seventeen

Change is Coming

After a little over a year of FCI Allenwood and having a set routine, I was told to pack it up; I was being transferred to the new penitentiary that was just built. Many inmates from Allenwood had hopes to be sent there, and quite a few had even put in for the transfer. Some were denied, some were accepted, and some were the luck of the draw as I was. Everything that I couldn't take with me I gave to Yusef and my celly Ace from New York. Typically, inmates downgrade from a penitentiary to an FCI medium to an FCI low and then off to a camp. I started at a medium and went up to a brand new USP Canaan, a penitentiary. I was shipped on the third busload into the pen. It had a much different feeling. Felt in comparison to being on a deserted island or being stranded in the forest without a map or compass. This high-security prison was built to house over twelve hundred inmates. It had six v-shaped buildings facing each other that housed inmates. Since the opening in 2005 when I was there, several inmates and even a guard has been murdered there. When I arrived, only one block had been opened so I knew or was familiar with most of the inmates from Allenwood. Everyone was saying that the guards were fresh meat and we as inmates had to set the tone and establish the rules for the guards to follow. Soon after I arrived, I heard someone yelling 'Pittsburgh' to someone. I assumed that wasn't regarding me because most of the inmates were from Allenwood. I looked and looked and then noticed a familiar face. It was 50 Run from my hood, somebody I knew very well, his little brother was 'Sprinkle Me'. 50 Run was in on the indictment with Doc Boog and Flash. We talked about everything, caught up on time, and started kicking it together. I didn't like the fact that it was five hours away. Allowing my wife to drive this trip wasn't happening. After just a mere three weeks, I was told to pack it up again! I had no idea what was going on. I didn't think I was being transferred. I left anything of prison value with 50 Run and my celly.

Twenty-six months in and I'm being escorted by US Marshalls onto the US Marshalls airplane again. This time I got onto the plane and seen familiar faces. First, it was the African Warrior, then Paula one of our runners, then Flash. I managed to get a seat somewhat across from Flash almost identical to the flight we took years before from Pittsburgh to ATL. US Marshalls made everyone keep the talk to a bare minimum. I managed to ask Flash what was going on and where he was coming from. He said he had been in Philly awaiting trial. Everyone was sentenced and, in their prisons, except him.

After the flight landed in Pittsburgh, several vans were waiting along with prison buses. Everyone shifted around once our inmate numbers were called. I couldn't believe what I was seeing! A twelve-passenger van with everyone I knew very well. Crump, Steph, African Warrior, Paula, and Larry Smith. I was unaware of what was taking place, but I was sure asking questions and wasn't getting many answers. Only time would tell, I guess.

Once we were at the County Jail, most numbers were called to exit the van except Flash and the African Warrior. I asked the marshals if Flash could get off at the county with us, but the request was denied. I said my goodbyes to my big homie as I exited the van.

In the county, I had numerous connects to guards to get what I needed. A call, extra clothes, bedding, single cell, whatever. I needed a phone call asap to call my wife to see what was going on. She knew everything being that Lancaster hired her to run his office. Yes, that was such a blessing in disguise for him and her. It worked out perfect. She was ambitious, smart, and trustworthy. He needed someone of her caliber. Despite her felony conviction, Lancaster started to know the real Monica. He had already known the real me.

In just a nick of time, the tables had turned, and she was in the courthouse postponing cases, filing motions, and writing briefs for Lancaster. God had turned a situation completely around in our favor. That became the talk of the courthouse and the city.

Once I got her on the line, she said she had heard Flash was preparing for trial and that there were over ten people that the government had brought in to testify and that ole boy would be the key witness against him. She had heard that his homie was pitching a fit and by no means did he want to do that. They always said that the last person on an indictment either was getting a big break from cooperation or completely the opposite and getting the stinky end of the deal. I was in my wife's ear asking her to call my attorney, to talk to her attorney and the DEA. I by no means was getting on the stand. And I wanted my time cut before I went back because I didn't want to keep leaving the prison I was at.

Well after a few weeks, I got the word. Flash took a plea just before the start of the trial. My wife made something happen because my attorney filed a motion for Rule 35b as it is known to most federal inmates and I had a hearing date for September. So I wouldn't be getting shipped back out until that day. Flash was sentenced to a harsh time that was totally inappropriate and way over the guidelines.

Once again, his supplier got a sentence less than two years and the judge sentenced him to 27 years. I was so sick to my stomach when I read that in the newspaper. There was no way 27 years in prison was justified for those charges. I wish I had been around him early on when we were arrested. I would've made sure he got on the same page as everyone else.

Once in the prison system, I learned that 85 percent cooperated but tried their best to hide it and the other 15 percent wished they had cooperated. The mafia code was broken a generation ago. When all the co-defendants are on the same page and all cooperate, everyone gets a sentence reduction from city to city, state to state, that is what was going on. The game was officially over.

After hearing and seeing how easy it was for someone to say your name without any actual proof and get away with it, that let me know that the system was rigged, and the government wasn't playing by the book. If you said a name they wanted to hear, they would accept your story and wrote them down as CS99 on somebody's paperwork.

Reub was sentenced to ten years. He was on phone calls throughout the whole wiretaps. He did beat the homicide charges though. Steph, Court Dog, and the drivers got less than five years. My artists were indicted after they took the stand in my defense at my detention hearing. The DEA came up with something talking about we took some drugs into Maine and 50G's apartment and they were aware and knew what it was. That was a complete lie. That was a low blow they were being railroaded. Everyone including the DEA knew that my artists didn't sell any drugs. Those kids were strictly about music. Rook was eventually caught after being on the run. He pled guilty and received a 10-year sentence.

September rolled around and it was time for my hearing. To my surprise, my mother wrote a letter to the judge as well as my cousin Pastor Jones. At my hearing, Lancaster even spoke on my behalf. The outpouring of love and support was such a blessing. Another thing in my favor was that my cousin Pastor Jones' daughter Michelle was the clerk for Judge Conti's courtroom. So, on September 5th, after serving 30 months of my sentence in federal custody, I was released! Completely unexpectedly! I had no clothes to wear from the courthouse, so Lancaster left out and purchased me an outfit and some sneakers to walk out of the federal courthouse in. I was in complete shock and all nerved out. I hadn't planned for this day at all. So now I had some decisions to make quick and in a hurry.

On my first day out, after leaving the courthouse, I ran into Blip Loc. He had owed me a few grand when I got arrested. He went in his pocket with no hesitation and gave me $3500 and a big hug. We talked briefly before he rolled out with his young boys.

I had read the scriptures in the book of James where if you submit yourself to God, wash your hands, purify your heart, and humble yourself before the Lord, He will lift you up. I realized at that moment, if it is the Lord's will, I would live to do this or that and that God opposes the proud but gives grace to the humble. I was finally free. Or was I? Yes, I was free from being in FBOP custody physically, but I wasn't free mentally as I thought, and along with five years of SUPERVISED release, I wasn't anywhere near free.

Water Walker on Concrete

Each of our conduct and actions had brought this upon each of us. Some were still in denial and hadn't accepted responsibility. At that point, God had laid us all down in our shame and let our disgrace cover us. We had all sinned against the Lord our God. Both we and our father before us from our youth 'til this very day, we had not obeyed the Lord our God. Walking out of that courthouse, I vowed to no longer follow the stubbornness of my evil heart. God has mercy on whom He chooses, and he hardens whom he wants to harden. Always know in your heart as a Christian that those who are called to serve the Lord may have to endure the rigors of poverty and deprivation. During those 30 months, I had learned to be courageous and not discouraged. If it was God's will with guidance from the Holy Spirit, I was walking on faith, not fear.

Once the word had got out in the streets that I was home, people were eager to see what I was up to. I had a few people come to me asking when I was getting back on. Yes, people were asking when I was going to start hustling that poison again because ‘things hadn’t been the same since I had gone to prison’. My response was things still won’t be the same because I’m not jumping back into that! I’m cool. I’m good. And you’re disrespecting me by even coming at me like that. Maybe it was the fact that everyone was used to people getting out of prison and jumping right back into the same situations as if they hadn’t learned one thing of value during their incarceration besides how to outsmart ‘themselves’ the next time around.

I decided to take one month to gather my thoughts before I decided what my next move would be. I certainly wanted my next move to be the best move and not a wasteful move. Fortunately, I was able to come home and not be desperate for money or housing as a lot of people are which leads to impatience and sometimes making the wrong move. I knew one thing that we both agreed to do was move again as my wife had moved back into the home we owned in the city. We had broken the lease for the luxury townhome we rented out but paid the remaining balance in full so it wouldn’t affect my family member’s credit that had signed the lease for us. Although I had received nothing less than a warm welcome from everyone I encountered, it was better to be safe for the wellbeing of my family. Anyone who knew me, or knew of me, knew that if they had come my way, they had better come correct and on point. That never changed.

Although I wasn't looking for any trouble, I was prepared for some resistance somewhere down the line. One thing I had to do was buy myself a vehicle being that we were down to one vehicle. Unsure of the type of work I would get into, I still needed a reliable source of transportation. I knew one thing for sure was that I wasn't getting anything flashy that would stick out as I had done previously over and over. I took a few thousand and purchased a Chevy. I took a few more thousand and rented another townhome in a predominantly white neighborhood. We decided to rent our home out and planned to never look back. I knew for sure that I wasn't getting back into the music business as it took money that I wasn't willing to spend. Anything I'd spend now would be calculated and well thought out along with a definite return. In the meantime, it was time to get a job to keep my parole officer off my back and to stop spending from my savings. The new obstacle was getting hired somewhere being a convicted felon.

I soon realized the struggle in the real world with being an African American with no college degree and a felony. Things were discouraging being that I was used to very rarely being told no and not having my way. I kept my head up high and filled out applications, one after another. With my hair braided up in cornrows, being stereotyped was certain and that didn't help the decision making after the interview nor with the first impression given. I still didn't understand that the things that seemed normal or small to me were seen by others in a different light.

After numerous attempts and over ten rejections, I finally landed my first job. The position required that I dress business casual (something that I wasn't used to) and use my vehicle to travel throughout the city and county selling (soliciting) toys, books, jackets, and the latest gadgets. We paired up in two's and targeted different areas going from establishments to the street to wherever a sale was possible.

I can recall calling my homie Slicc and stopping past his home dressed in my work attire and soft walkers. He looked like, "Bro, what up. I know them folks didn't change you up like that." My response was, "Bro, they ain't playing right. They tryna lock us up forever. The game is over, Bro. I already told you that your girl's little brother tried to book you already. He's working with the FEDs. He wore a wire then ran off, Bro. You better fall back. Little Corey working with them. Now buy a couple of hundred dollars in toys off me." He bought the toys, but he didn't listen to the other part! Less than a year later, he was indicted with his cousins and a few people from California and a cartel. He was charged with distribution of 2,000 kilos. He fought for his life though. He represented himself at trial and was convicted of distributing just five kilos. I guess representing himself was a good move. Pleading guilty would have sent him away forever. Instead, he received a twenty-year sentence. Had he stopped when I had told him to, he may have made it out the game before the game made out on him!

Although I could have connected with him and jumped right back in on a major scale, I remained humble and continued working a job that paid mere chump change. That was the last day I saw Slicc. Now we keep in touch through emails via federal prison.

After two months of doing that work, I decided to go through a temp agency and landed a job just minutes away from my home building steel girders for bridges. I learned to weld while working the graveyard shift. I also learned to grind and sweep shop floors!

In less than two years, I had a 401K plan saved up that was looking pretty good and met a whole different group of people along the way. I had never known anything about a 401K. My 401K was stacking tens of thousands at a time and keeping it very far away from a bank. A change had come. Adjusting was still taking some time, but I had managed to weather the storm. There were plenty of opportunities, propositions, and temptations along the way. God never said it would be easy, but I recognized Satan's work now. Even on the job, the devil worked through other individuals to try and throw me off my square.

If I Can Change, You Can

We managed to purchase a few more homes along the way. A move that has always been rewarding. God had a plan and it included him blessing us with another child. We welcomed a baby boy into the world in 2008. Through a mutual friend of my wife's, she was introduced to a Jewish family that owned numerous buildings and real estate in the Squirrel Hill area of Pittsburgh. The couple was elderly and was on the verge of selling their properties. The mutual friend had been employed by this Jewish family. However, he had let the properties he managed go completely down the drain. Knowing our capabilities, he reached out as a first and last resort with hopes that we could change things around and convince them not to sell the properties. I was employed in building bridges, but Monica had the time to make things happen. We put our heads together and came up with a few resources. I got my brother-in-law involved and got him a job being he had handy hands all his life of me knowing him. We also knew a flooring guy that had started doing our floors and carpet when we would purchase homes. He was willing to work also. The Jewish couple wanted me to come on board so my wife and I could work as a team, they made an offer that was well above the rate I was making building bridges. The Jewish family had become our family. They taught us so much along the way and treated us like family, welcoming us into their homes for dinner on Shabbat. They lived the complete opposite of what we were used to on the weekends.

On the weekends, we wanted to go out and party and spend the money we worked so hard all week to make. While in their community from Sunset Friday to the fall of darkness on Saturday, they studied, prayed, and spent time in their homes with family. That was something I admired and soon followed similarly. I figured I could at least save money if I didn't look for the party or the latest happening being that it was the weekend that was something that grew on me more over the years.

Financially, I learned the importance of credit and all the ins and outs in the real estate business. I believe God had put that family in our lives at the right time. This very day and time, I can call them for advice or if I need anything else. Those were some of the most wonderful people I had ever met.

With the guidance of them teaching us how to be super disciplined, we acquired several other properties of our own. It was then that I paid close attention to the handymen we had hired to flip the apartments. We decided to pull all floors, cabinets, and bathrooms and start fresh and change the carpet to wood. As soon as we finished a place, it was already rented. Monica soon had a waiting list. She turned fifty percent vacant into one hundred percent full, with a waiting list. I caught on to the remodeling and maintenance side of things pretty fast. Soon I knew everything there was to know about a home and building.

The Jewish family was so nice that they sent me to school for HVAC. It was during that time I became knowledgeable with circuits. Blessings were being poured onto me in abundance. My mother said she had covered me. I certainly believed it because I had lived it and witnessed it year after year in more than one way. The Jewish family I knew had a mission to be a light unto the nations and to exemplify the covenant with God as described in the Torah. I was covered from all angles. My mother had re-dedicated her life to the Lord in the early 90s. she completed a year of study and training for a leadership class and in 2006 answered her call to the ministry, preached her first sermon and was licensed by Pastor Jones in April 2008. She's a graduate of an outreach Bible school as well. She served in various capacities including youth and adult Sunday School teaching, Bible study instructor, and senior choir member. She was a part of the praise team, the helping Hands Gospel choir, the Pastor's Aide, Lydia's Place Prison Ministry, leadership training class, initiated the first women's conference which birthed the Women of Purpose ministry. She also started the turkey giveaway that is now known as the Harvest Baskets. She has accepted her Prophetic Gifting on January 21, 2018, at the direction of the Holy Spirit, Prophet Bill Moody confirmed her to the Office of a Prophet by the laying on of the hands. And on November 18th, 2018 she went before the council and received the laying on of hands and certificate to become Reverend Chaffin. She currently heads the Citizen Police Review Board in Duquesne, PA where it all started.

At one of the very first meetings, she was stopped in the hallway of the City Hall building by the newly elected chief of police. The officer approached her and asked, "Are you Clabo's mother?" She replied, "Yes, I am." He then went on to say after sticking his chest out, "I'm Officer Wannabee I used to be a DEA agent. I'm the one who arrested your son." She replied, "Well, thank you because he has served his time and changed his life completely around. He doesn't loaf with the same friends and has been very successful in his endeavors. So thank you again!" She has encountered him on numerous occasions afterward and he has even tried to mention my name again to her up until she shut him down. She told him, "Look, every time you see me, I don't want to hear nothing about my son. That was over fifteen years ago and that's not what his life consists of now." I told my mother that was probably the largest case that he was ever a part of but thank you, Mom, for shutting him down and now being a part of investigating his practices now!

Doors are opening up. God sent his Jewish children to look out for and teach the man who had gone out on faith and trusted in the Lord's word. I declared an end to my warfare. I made peace with my portion this day. The enemy never bows his knee willingly, but he will bow.

The Dunamis flowing through me brought me out of every captivity in my life. Doors had opened, the works of men erected to restrict me will fall out to my benefit as God will turn the enemy upon himself, making the enemy his own worst enemy.

God said nothing shall move me. The scoffer should be silenced, the mocker will be brought to shame. I took refuge in His Name to prepare to go forth into the wealthy place. I will not be moved by the threat that comes in daylight nor the intimidation that lurks in thc darkness!

Chapter Eighteen

Never Could Have Made It

The kids were enjoying the fast track line in Disney World. It was just 3:30 pm on a Friday and I was exhausted, sweaty, and tired already. I had been up half the night due to my eighteen-year-old son leaving the hotel with someone I didn't know from a can of paint. He stayed out until 2 am with a cell phone that the battery had supposedly died according to him. When he finally did show up, my adrenaline pumped so heavy that it was hours before I slept. Sitting with Ty on the beach, my phone rang. When I answered, a soft-spoken lady was asking if she could speak with me addressing me by my government name. "Yes, speaking. How can I help you?" I replied. "Good afternoon sir, I wanted to offer you the position you applied for." The conversation went on for a couple of minutes. I hung the phone up and said to my wife, "They offered me that position, also. Both places called back today. They both want me."

I had gone from not being able to get one job years ago to now multiple companies seeking to hire me at the same time. The one place I had interviewed with had a story behind it. That place was the very same place

I lived when I got indicted and was sent to prison. The very same place I now have the keys to at this time because I am the technician on call 24 hours. I called Ms. Mel back and asked if they had run just a state background check on me or if they did a federal one as well. I knew that nothing would come up under any state check as I had no state convictions. But if they had run a federal background check, they'd see that I had a felony and I even had a deeper story that they might want to know about before offering me the position. She asked what that story was, and I told her my old address and said I was arrested from that location. But even in breaking the lease, "I paid the remainder of what was owed in full," I stated jokingly. She exclaimed I'll call you back shortly after I talk with some people. She certainly called me back and said, "Clabo, everyone deserves a second chance. Thank you for your honesty. When can you start?"

I started the following week. Going back into the townhome I had been taken out of in handcuffs years earlier was a bit strange the first time, but I was happy to be on the other end now. Soon after, I started my own General Contracting business and continued buying and renting houses out in the inner cities of Pittsburgh.

My oldest son joined the Armed Forces and started his own family. My oldest daughter lives in North Carolina and has ventured off on her own mission. My youngest daughter attends college and is pursuing her degree in education. My youngest son, Ty, is laid back with the same personality as I had before I jumped off the porch at eleven years old. He enjoys basketball year-round. I now have four grandchildren of my own from my oldest two children.

My brother was arrested and found guilty of conspiring in a major cocaine ring in 2015. He was sentenced to eleven years. According to the books, he won't get out of federal prison until he is almost 60 years old.

My sister has worked for the IRS for the last 22 years.

Tee survived nearly 17 years in the game without getting busted until just a year ago. He received a lenient sentence due to health issues.

Rook got out after doing the 10 years then was indicted again within a year of being released. He was convicted again and sentenced to another 10 years, which would amount to over thirty years total for him.

Flash is now Brotha T. He is 17 years into a 27-year sentence. He and I communicate via email and text. He has become a born-again Christian. He is not ashamed of the gospel of Christ. He is steadfast and rich in the word. He says the word is piercing the depths of his soul for a unique purpose and the living testimony that lives within him.

Steph moved to Maryland and is a successful trainer with his own gym.

Crump is still in Pittsburgh doing who knows what, with God knows who and still catching cases.

Doc is married and still resides in Georgia and is doing well raising two children of his own.

Reub is in Pittsburgh living his life to the fullest.

Rodney was gunned down in the city.

CY is back in the hood where it all started with his high school alums Tone B and a few other 1994 grads.

Bowie City was murdered on the very same street that we shared our apartment together in Duquesne.

Look through what is going on around you and not just at the surface. Truth heard the first time often produces a negative reaction. Set aside vain opinion and the convenience of your own suppositions. Men plan but God directs. Think it's not strange or a hard thing for all his pathways are peace, even when we don't know the end from the beginning. I was told to just rest and trust that he is authoring in me.

Peace and Blessings to all. Corinthians 5:17 "Therefore, if anyone is in Christ, the new creation has come. The old has gone." The new is here and finally free!

Chapter Nineteen

Finally Free

The Lord has called upon me to forgive, release, and bless. I forgave those who had occasioned offense in my life. I have released them from expectations that I have not lived up to. I refuse to be small-minded. I refuse to walk in rejection, anger, or opinion. This is a new day. This has been a growing up season for me. The root of bitterness never languishes. It thrives until it dominates every area and every relationship of your life. It is a plant that we cannot afford to allow to encumber the precious ground God has given us. Let it go. Forget the past. I extend to others the compassion that I desire to receive from God's hand. I choose to walk in a path of peace and righteousness. I am a seed sower, not a dealer. I am not subject to the seed. However, the seed is subject to me. I was called and ordained by the work of the cross to be a lord over my harvest. What that means is I can call for crop failure, that is what repentance is all about. Repentance is the primary work of the first principles of Christ. I took advantage of the Lord's opportunity that he extended to me to repent of hasty doings and bitter judgments.

The harsh decisions of the past don't define my journey ahead. I am finally free from small-minded thinking, ill intentions, free from worrying whether the police are coming to kick in my door. I was measuring life from earthly ways, health, wealth, and power. God will take you through the wilderness to awake you to the glorification of his mighty work.

It was God who healed my mother from the devil's work and product of the addiction to heroin and it didn't require one day in rehab for her to be delivered. Not one day! Minister Chaffin was delivered by the Holy Spirit. It was he who had his hands on me throughout the temporal changeable situations that seemed so big. He is the God that spun the cosmos off his fingers across the expanse of creation! I felt the full weight of his power and glory burst into my life and completely reshape it. Meditate on that!

Set your mind on his limitlessness, not on limitation. What we set our attention on sets the preamble for what happens next in our life. The man of sin will die, and the new creation will stand up in authority and righteousness. The crooked path will be made straight and the painful road to be 'yoke easy and burden light'. Spiritually I am finally free. Physically, emotionally, and psychologically as well. I refuse to be bound by Satan's work.

God said he would be the Father to the Fatherless. He said I was coming out of the fire. He told me the heat and pressure surrounding me would not even tinge the garments of my soul with the slightest smell of smoke. The chaos and clamor around me will only result in the promotion and refinement of my unfolding purpose in life. I was willing to walk out of captivity. The chains have fallen so that I walk onward in the calling of my life.

Now is the time. I won't look to the right or the left. Some will never understand. So I never seek the approval of others for what God has spoken so openly regarding me. I came out of the place of restriction, laid aside the grave clothes that only had me bound by the carnality of wrong choices.

I was set free this day to embrace and receive my inheritance. The associations of the past are dissolved, and a new tribe awaits. They will march and go forth not spearing one another or treading upon one another but hastening and helping each other toward the ultimate fulfillment of the conquest at hand.

Open your heart says the Father, letting go of the past and pressing into a new day that is dawning in your life and watch you be set FINALLY FREE!

About the Author

Tennille Chaffin was born and raised in Pittsburgh Pa where he succumbed to the streets at eleven years old. Growing up in government housing where he lived a poverty-stricken childhood, fatherless with a mother addicted to heroin he spent 15 years in the streets before finding his spiritual father. He's sharing this story with hopes to inspire others and shed light on the untold truths about his life experiences Deep in the game, a TRUTH that most would be ashamed to speak about! Riveting, inspiring. Shocking, a gut-wrenching true story.

Connect with Tennille on Instagram @clabo100 or email at Tennille.chaffin@yahoo.com for business inquiries only

Made in the USA
Lexington, KY
27 November 2019